Riding the
Spirit Wind

Riding the Spirit Wind

Stories of Shamanic Healing

John Myerson
&
Robert Greenebaum

LifeArts
PRESS

Address inquiries to:

LifeArts Press
64 Lexington Street
Framingham, MA 01702
(508) 879-3002
Or visit www.life-arts.com.
E-mail: info@life-arts.com

Printed in the United States of America.

First Edition 2003
ISBN 0-9744414-0-6
Riding the Spirit Wind: Stories of Shamanic Healing
John Myerson & Robert Greenebaum

PLEASE NOTE

The cases described in this book are composites.
They have been deliberately combined in order to protect
John Myerson's patients' rights of confidentiality and privacy.
No client found in this book corresponds to
any actual person, living or dead.

Dedication

This book is dedicated to the souls of the ancestors
whose love has always sustained me.

In memory of my Father
Henry M. Myerson
1910-1985
May his memory be blessed for ever and ever.

I am standing on a high rock overhang, overlooking the woods. It is
autumn, cool, and clear air with the first touch of winter. The leaves have
changed and everywhere I look is orange, red and yellow. I call on the souls
of the ancestors. As they come, I feel a great opening in my chest, I feel the
connection of their love and I ride the spirit wind. My heart extends out
over the woods to all living beings and the universe. At the same time I feel
strong and overwhelmed by a feeling of oneness.

I feel, as I spread my arms to the universe, open and vulnerable as I offer
you this work. It is my sincere hope it will be of use to you. This is my first
such offering and I feel a great sense of humility and gratitude to be able to
offer this work, and a sense of profound thanks to all those who have
worked hard with me to make this possible. To all those who have had the
courage to make the journey with me, I dedicate this work.

John Myerson

Acknowledgements

John Myerson

I would like to acknowledge all the people who have helped me on my Way. I have learned from you all. My profound thanks to Robert Greenebaum: without his vision, drive and compassion, this book would never have been completed. To Maureen Stuart Roshi, Paul Gallagher, James Tin Yau So, Dennis Reynolds, Ira Fritz, Helen Gitkind and Natasha. Thanks to Maria Hodgdon for keeping me in line and Judy Robbins for being you. To the men: Bruce Berlent, Mark Halperin, Andy Osborne, Peter Ostrow, Paul Weisman and Phil Weinstein for all your love and support these many years. All my love to my wife Laura, who for over 30 years has put up with it all.

Robert Greenebaum

In bringing these stories of John's Healing Ways to light I would first like to thank the individuals who have had the courage to live them. Secondly, I offer profound gratitude to John Myerson for the opportunity to participate in this project. Additional teachers whom I can never thank enough include Amy Lew, Dennis Reynolds, Roger Woolger, Joel Karp, and Barry Schrage. To my wife Jamie: I offer you my love, and my gratitiude for your support throughout this project and in so many other ways.

Also, I send appreciation and gratitude to all my readers on this project: Joan Cleary, Bob Friedman, Jamie Greenebaum, Amelia Kinkade, Dorri Li, Deborah Macchi, Bill Manning, Paula Mastroberardino, Beth Menczer, Ellen Pfeifer, Rob Randall, Judy Robbins, Judy Seidl, Christine Sugarman, and Lisbeth Tanz—with special thanks to Jamie Greenebaum and Deborah Macchi for invaluable editorial assistance.

Table of Contents

Preface

Pain. Anguish. Rage. Fear. Shame. Loneliness. Hopelessness. These, and other difficult feelings, are an integral part of our lives. Everyone experiences these, to one degree or another, at one time or another. And each of us has many problems. In the course of our days and nights we may have enormous difficulties, seemingly beyond help. Perhaps we even feel that the world is nothing but problems and painful feelings. We may yearn for relief. We may pray for it. We may even be brought to our knees and beg for it. What is unquestionable is that the paths of the heart are many and diverse, and ultimately each of us has our own road to walk.

As we walk our individual paths, it may happen that we come into contact with someone who helps us. Maybe a teacher in grade school takes notice of us. As adults, possibly we have a friend who can help us. But, sometimes there seems to be no one who can understand our pain, and help us deal with our extreme difficulties. To whom would we turn in such circumstances. Do we feel that our physician can help? Is surgery appropriate, or medication? Are we beyond the reach of contemporary medicine? Then will our religious leader help us, if we have one? Do we even know how to pray beyond recitation? Possibly our problem is seemingly unsolvable by even all the might of our medical technology, and our community religion seems inadequate to help us. Should we give up at this point? Is there really nowhere else to turn?

You may find answers to such questions in this book. Here we are presenting the stories of a number of people who have undergone a healing experience that has changed their lives. Each has faced what appeared to them to be a total impasse. These are all quite ordinary individuals, many with no or little previous knowledge or experience of the healing processes which helped them move on from their dilemmas. One of the extraordinary aspects of these stories is how far from the expected direction the needed answers came. These stories demonstrate that each of us is, in fact, much more complex than even our most fantastic imaginings, or our most detailed descriptions of who we think we are, and what we think it means to live a life. The world in which we live is, in fact, a much stranger and more magical place than we have been led to believe by our parents, teachers, technologists, religions, and the press. Whether we wish to or not, we all live in this world, which is pre-existent of our great contemporary societies. And in this world healers do also live, who can connect with the actual hidden forces which affect us all.

If you read this book with an open mind and an open heart, in it you may find hope.

Robert Greenebaum

Authors' Note

In recent years there has been great interest in the subject of "Shamanism"—and especially in "Shamanic powers." Famous scholarly anthropological works have been published on the subject of indigenous traditional Shamanism and have been widely quoted in many contexts. Authors of more popularly oriented books and articles have primarily taken the viewpoint that "native" cultures hold the keys to shamanic realms, powers, and healing, sometimes characterized as sorcery. These authors have been particularly impressed with South American forest peoples who use psychotropic herbs, with the Australian aboriginal Dreamtime, as well as with native North American cultures of the southwestern United States and Mexico which use peyote to achieve altered states of consciousness. It is primarily the magical otherness and perceived exotic journeying experiences which the authors dwell upon—an updated version of the "Magical Mystery Tour" of an earlier generation of spiritual seekers which concentrated primarily on the practices and beliefs of major religions of the East. Further, the concepts of journeying to other worlds, encountering various space-time continuums, other universes and related ideas, have been popularized through fantasy and science fiction literature, film, television, and computer games.

All these various explorations of modes of reality—and the nature of human consciousness and its boundaries—yearn towards an understanding and personal experience of our spirituality. All have in common an interest in deep, shared spiritual experience that is also an aspect of this book. However, in contrast to these scholarly and recreational presentations, the primary focus of this book is our position that shamanic experience performs an essential function in all healing processes, in all people worldwide.

This is not a how-to book on shamanic practice, but a description of the healing process from various points of view. Of particular interest to readers will be the stories of healing told from the patient's viewpoint. These stories are based on actual case histories, and have been developed with attention to presenting authentic personal experiences of shamanic healing as practiced by John Myerson. Each story is accompanied by an interview with John Myerson addressing related ideas and issues. In addition, we are including background information on John Myerson in the Appendix interview, and a list of suggested reading by each author. We hope that you will benefit from our multi-faceted approach to this intriguing and controversial subject.

The Authors

Chapter 1

Learning to Love

Catherine

Part 1

I was in my car at a stoplight, the first one in line. I had to make a left turn. The light changed. I turned my head to the right to check the traffic. OK. Then I looked left, and pain shot out from behind my left ear, and down my left arm, freezing me on the spot. The car horns started at once, since I was blocking the intersection, but I couldn't move. After a moment the pain subsided, and I made the turn and got the hell out of Dodge. This was not an unusual occurrence for me. This excruciating neck pain had been with me now for the better part of a year.

I didn't have any kind of accident, or fall and hit my head, or anything like that. But every time I'd turn a certain way I'd get a jolt that would just about put me down on the floor. The rest of the time it was a dull ache. Some days I could hardly drive to work. I'd also get pains up and down my arms. I tried everything, starting with my doctor, and later I saw an orthopedist, and then I got a second orthopedic opinion. There was nothing they could really do for me except prescribe medication to relax the muscles in my neck. It didn't really do much for the pain. Then I had physical therapy. That barely worked, too, so I tried several chiropractors, and later, massage therapists. I'd get a little temporary relief, but mostly not much. I was at my wit's end about it. It was just wearing me out. At that point I was complaining to my friend, Will, and he gave me John Myerson's name and number. Will said in his best lawyer's voice, "Why don't you try acupuncture? What have you got to lose? And this guy's good. I know him."

I called John and made an appointment for the following week. I'll admit I was somewhat apprehensive, but he sounded sincere on the phone and he told me, "I think I'll be able to help you." That was something new in the midst of all the pain. It wasn't the only thing I thought about that week, but I was looking forward to the appointment with some sense of hope.

I parked in front of John's building and went in to the first floor waiting room. It was pretty plain, like any other office in the residential neighborhood. Kind of an ordinary building, really. Since I was a bit early, I picked up a magazine to read while waiting. Just then a tall woman came down the stairs, and as she left I heard a male voice say, "Catherine? Come on up." It was John himself. It surprised me. There was no receptionist. I went up the flight of stairs and down the short hall to John's office. He was standing there to usher me in. "Come in, Catherine," he smiled.

His office was quite small, with a desk at one end, and a couch and his chair at the other. Primitive art adorned the walls. It was neat, but not too neat. John motioned me to sit on the couch, and I complied.

"Catherine," he began, still smiling at me, "tell me about it. I mean the neck pain. Let's see what we can do to help you."

"Well, I've had some kind of neck pain for years, probably since my early thirties," I told him. "But in the last several months, maybe a half-year, it's gotten really bad. I've been to a number of doctors, and a physical therapist, and even had massage, with no real relief."

"Where's the pain?"

"Here, on my left side," I answered, turning to show him the area.

"Any other places?"

"Yes, sometimes I get shooting pains in my arms and hands. Nobody can tell me what it is."

"Tell me about yourself." John opened his arms wide, and I suddenly felt safe for the first time in ages.

"OK, John. I'm 43. I live alone, but I have a steady guy. I run a social services organization in Boston. And I attend night school at BU. And I like the occasional opera. My job has lots of responsibility and meetings. I hardly ever see my boyfriend, Roy. My commute to and from my job in Boston is close to an hour each way. I get home after night school, around ten-thirty, and I still have a few household chores to do. Then I go to bed. But it's always the same. I have so many thoughts going around in my head that I can't get to sleep. Mostly it's problems from work, and sometimes things about Roy. Often it's the same thing just repeating itself over and over and over. I finally drift off to sleep early in the morning, and then the alarm goes off, and it all starts again. It never stops."

"Sounds like a lot of commitments."

"I guess. But lately this neck pain has really been getting in my way."

"I'm sure it has. Well, for today, I'd like to give you an acupuncture treatment. Come in to the treatment room."

John beckoned to me to go through another door into a small room off his main office. There were a lot of bookshelves and more interesting decorations, and there was a treatment table. He set a stepstool next to it so I could get onto the table. I lay down on the table, and John began the treatment. He told me, "Catherine, have you ever had acupuncture before?" I shook my head. "Well, no, I didn't think so," he continued. You probably won't even feel the needles. They're disposable, by the way, for reasons of health safety. The treatment should relax you. You'll probably fall asleep."

After placing the needles, he started some quiet music and left the room. The next thing I knew, John was coming through the door as I was awakening. He turned off the music and removed the needles. To my surprise, it had been almost forty-five minutes. As I got up from the table I realized that I felt refreshed, and even a little bouncy. We went back out to his office.

He motioned me back to the couch where I had been sitting before. "Catherine," he said to me with great sincerity and a little chuckle, "you've got to give yourself a break. I'd like you to come back in a week for another treatment. In the meantime, try to take it a little bit easier. Maybe do a little less. OK?"

I agreed, "OK John," but I was dubious. On the other hand, the treatment did make me feel better. After arranging my next appointment, I left, and as I did I realized that John hadn't put acupuncture needles anywhere near my neck. "How odd," I thought.

For the next several days I actually did feel somewhat more relaxed, but by the weekend I was in a tizzy again, and as my appointment with John came closer, I just seemed to get all wrapped up in everything. My neck was really bad again.

"Come on up, Catherine," John invited me from the top of the stairs. As I sat down he asked, "So, how are you doing?"

"My neck is killing me!" And I told him my news from the week, about a few frustrations at my job, and how my classes were going.

"You need to slow down, Catherine." John told me. "You're always rushing from one thing to another. You need to give yourself some breathing room, literally. I'd like you to try some meditation. Have you ever done it?"

"No."

"Well, it's really very simple. You sit in a chair with your feet on the floor and your hands in your lap. You don't need any special hand positions. Just keep your back straight without tensing up. Breathe lightly in through your nose and out through your mouth. Count each time you exhale. Like this: Exhale. Count 'one.' Inhale. Count 'and.' Exhale. 'Two.' Inhale. 'And.' Exhale. 'Three.' And so forth. Let's try it together." I tried it with him. It was pretty easy.

"Now as you're doing this, just try to let your thoughts go," he continued. "Maybe you could spend five to ten minutes in the morning, and again in the evening, meditating like this. How about it, Catherine?"

"OK, John, I'll try it."

Then I had my second acupuncture treatment, which again seemed to relax me in ways I don't think I had ever felt before.

"See you next week, Catherine," John said lightly as I went through the door. I heard him calling the next person to come up as I left the building. I noticed that I really felt that someone finally cared deeply about my welfare. This was another new feeling. "I'm really glad I came to see John," I thought. "Maybe I'll get through this yet."

I tried the meditation. I probably managed three or four minutes once a day, but I found that I liked it. I just couldn't do it for very long. I felt like I was wasting time, letting important things go undone. And I realized that my neck didn't hurt as much. The pain was still there, but the really sharp, debilitating part was certainly lessened. "From two acupuncture treatments?" I asked myself. "Can that be true?"

I asked John about it.

"You know, Catherine," he stated, "the real problem with your neck is not physical. The treatments I am giving you are not treatments for neck pain. I'm treating you to release the pent-up emotional energy, and to allow you to relax into a healing state. It's temporary, because you habitually block the energy in your neck, which causes pain, and your habit pattern reestablishes itself after a few days. But, I think the results will become permanent after a few more treatments. How's the meditation working for you?"

"I actually like it," I told him. "I never thought about it before. I mean, no one ever taught me how to do it. And I can't do it for more than a few minutes, before I have to get up and go do something else. I just find the same thoughts repeating themselves. I can only take so much of that!"

"The purpose of meditation is to learn how to let your thoughts go about their own business, Catherine. In your case, you tend to let yourself get carried away by a few thoughts that compel you to take the action they indicate. You get into trouble because you let these thoughts dictate to you. When you meditate this week, just try to let the thoughts float by. Don't stop them, and see if they just leave by their own accord."

"It sounds like you're saying that the thoughts are alive.".

"In a certain sense they are very alive. But you are not your thoughts. You are very much more than that. Actually, your thoughts don't even belong to you. Let them go. Try it and see what happens."

I was actually horrified. "But John, what you're saying is awful. I mean, that my thoughts are not mine?"

"That's right. Thoughts are like fish in the ocean, Catherine. There are lots of little thoughts on the surface. Then there are other thoughts in the shallow water. There are bigger thoughts still, in the deeper parts. And there are huge thoughts, like whales in the very depths. Where do these thoughts come from? We don't know. Where do they go? We don't know. If you know the answers to these questions you will be the first person ever to do so. Isn't what I am saying true?"

I thought about it for a moment, frantically trying to maintain my equilibrium. I actually felt dizzy. I just couldn't accept that my thoughts didn't belong to me. But, on the other hand, I didn't know where they came from or went. Logically, how could they be mine? "John," I said, "you're scaring the piss out of me!"

"Don't worry about it, Catherine!" John laughed in a big booming laugh.

It was infectious; I couldn't help but start laughing myself. After all, I was already starting to obsess about that!

"Just try to let your thoughts float by when you're meditating this week. See if you can let them go their own way. Just give it a try, and if you feel dizzy, stop and come back to it later. Let's go get you a treatment."

I left that time in a daze. First of all, during the acupuncture I had fallen into the deepest sleep I could ever remember, and I was still a little groggy. And second, I was still reeling from our conversation. "But, you know what?" I thought. "Your neck doesn't hurt at all! Amazing!"

So I figured that something was working, even though I really didn't understand what. I kept on with the meditation, still unable to do it for very long at a time, and went for my acupuncture treatments for the next few weeks. I loved talking to John. And the acupuncture treatments were a real oasis of calm in the midst of the storm.

"Catherine," John was asking me at my next visit, "how do you feel now?"

"My neck has stopped hurting."

"I already know about that. What I'm asking you is HOW DO YOU FEEL? You know, are you happy, sad, up, down, whatever?"

"I don't know."

"You don't?"

"No. And stop bugging me about it."

"You don't have any feelings?"

"OF COURSE I HAVE THEM!"

"So, how do you feel?"

"There. See, you're doing it again. Leave me alone!"

John was looking at me with a calm little smile, not saying anything. I suddenly realized that he loved me. Really loved me. I could almost see the love coming from him. It felt like waves. I burst into tears. I couldn't stop crying for a long time. He didn't interrupt me, or come over and put his arm around me, but I could still feel him loving me. Finally I was done. I looked up at him.

"Catherine, how do you feel?"

"HAPPY!" And I was sobbing again.

"You see, Catherine, your feelings connect you to things. They connect you to people. They connect you to the universe. They connect you to yourself. One of the reasons you go running around doing so many things is because you don't want to feel. But you're just chasing your own tail. To really live, you need to really feel. How are you feeling now?"

"OK." I was drained.

"I think we'll skip your acupuncture treatment today. You've done enough."

I suppose that I could have stopped seeing John any time. My neck no longer hurt. But I felt I was getting something more important than even relief from that awful pain. Somehow John knew me deep down, where I didn't even know myself. He was the first person I had known who really understood me. I realized that he was helping me become me. I wanted more.

And I got it a few weeks later. It set me back on my heels.

John was sitting in his usual chair, and I was in mine. "Catherine," he began, "I want to teach you how to connect with the souls."

"Souls?" I said, my head snapping up. "What was this?" I asked myself, "some Satanist cult?"

"I want you to learn how to connect with the souls that will help you heal through love," he continued.

"It sounds scary," I answered, looking at him with my head cocked to one side, more than a little dismayed.

"You might be scared, but it's only your upbringing talking. You know that I'm not talking about that kind of souls. I'm talking about the helping souls. You know, angels, if you want to call them that. Here's some paper, write down what I tell you exactly. After you meditate, and your mind is clear, I want you to read this prayer. You don't have to say it out loud. Just try it and see what happens. Be patient."

"What's this all about, John," I asked indignantly. "I feel like you're doing something to me."

"Well, actually, Catherine, haven't I been doing something to you all along? Isn't that why you came to see me in the first place?"

He had me there. What was I so upset about?

"It's this 'soul' thing, John. It scares me."

"It's only that you're unfamiliar with it, Catherine. It's new. You know, I bet if you think about it you believe that you have a guardian angel. Do you?"

"I guess I do," I answered suspiciously.

"Well, this prayer just gets you in touch with your guardian angel, or angels."

"Who are they?"

"It's another one of those things. We don't really know who they are. But we know that they do help us. And we know that this prayer gets us in touch with them. I'd like you to try it. Just read it to yourself when you are calm after you meditate."

"OK, I'll try it." But I was still scared.

John dictated the prayer, and I wrote it down on the paper he gave me, the back of some flyer he had available on a clipboard.

He finished, and looked at me. "Can you feel them?" he asked.

I was surprised. I thought I could feel something, like a mild tingling, or a vague pressure in the room.

"That's the souls, or as you would call them, the angels," John stated, smiling.

I had gone very quiet. "You mean they're here now?" I asked, incredulously.

"Yes, when they are called, they must come. They were called by my dictation, now they are here. To help."

"It sounds terrible, John," I said. "It sounds like they are slaves."

"Well, in a sense, I suppose you could say that is true. However, they don't seem to mind. In fact, I think they like to be called to help."

"I'm still uncomfortable with this," I told him.

"Just give it a try for a week," he said, smiling again. "I think you'll like the results."

I left, this time with some misgivings. However, John had helped me a lot. He had been completely trustworthy, and there was really no reason for me not to trust him now. Actually, now that I thought about it, it was kind of exciting, this thing with the angels. I decided to try it for a week, as John had requested.

At home that evening, I did my meditation, letting my thoughts drift where they would, as I had learned, letting them go. When I became calm, I took out the paper and read the prayer to myself. Nothing happened. I read it again. Still nothing. Then again. I waited. Nothing.

The next morning I repeated the same thing. This time, did I feel something? I wasn't sure. I kept at it for several days. Then one evening, I thought I felt something. Maybe a stirring. Maybe a little more energy in the room.

Maybe a little more...I don't know exactly what. I kept at it all week. I thought, "Well, maybe I'm just not good at this."

My next visit, I asked John, "What are you supposed to feel with this prayer, John?"

His answer, "Let's try it together."

Neither of us said anything out loud. I said the prayer—I knew it by heart now—in my mind. John said, "Do you feel it?"

"What?"

"Can you feel the difference?"

Suddenly I was aware that the air in the room was scintillating with energy. It seemed that the air was actually a substance that flickered and shone with thousands of little lights. Then it faded away.

John was smiling. "Just keep at it, Catherine. I think you have a talent for this."

I did keep at it. Sometime during the third week I began to feel calmer, even cheerful, which, to say the least, was unusual for me. I didn't get any "messages," but I did start to feel more connected to everything around me. I actually started to look forward to the next day.

I asked John, "Is this just beginner's luck?"

"No, I don't think so, Catherine. I really think you have an aptitude for this work." He was smiling again as he answered me. It wasn't smug or anything, just happy. "You know," he continued, "you can use this ability to help other people, too, not just yourself."

"How can I do that?" I asked him, apprehensive again.

"First, call the souls or angels for yourself as you've learned already. Then just call them for the other person."

"Like who would I do this for?"

"Anyone. Maybe someone you know who is going through a hard time. Or someone in the hospital. Or just a friend who might need a little lift. Or someone in an auto accident you pass. Anyone you choose. You see, Catherine, you've come out the other side. At first you needed my help. Now you can offer help to others."

I was literally stunned. I still viewed myself as John's "patient." Now he was telling me that I didn't need him anymore. And, beyond that, that I could help other people, too.

"I just can't believe what you're telling me, John. I can do this for anyone I want, and it will work?" I asked.

"Just try it, Catherine. And I don't think you need to keep coming for acupuncture, unless you want to. We're finished for now. Call me anytime, I'll always be available for you. And stay out of trouble." He laughed that huge laugh, as he showed me to the door. Then I was out the door, down the stairs and walking to my car. It was over. Or was it?

I continued to practice the meditation and the prayer. I tried to help people I knew. And even people I didn't know. I did, in fact, feel more connected to everything. And I kept in touch with John, and shared my experiences with him on the phone. I thought I'd never visit him in his office again. But I was wrong about that.

As time went on, however, John would occasionally invite me to one of his "drumming sessions." These were half-day retreats where a group of a dozen to eighteen or so people would gather with him and his drumming session partner Dan. They would create a protected space to explore the shamanic realms via meditation, acupuncture, and music. First John would lead a meditation to get us to relax and start looking within, possibly preceded by some singing or chanting. Then we would lie down on our mats, and he and Dan, also an acupuncturist as well as a master percussionist, would give us acupuncture to relax us further. This usually consisted of several acupuncture needles gently inserted in one ear, one hand, and one foot. They were painless, and besides, I was used to this already. As we would lie there, sort of drifting, Dan would begin a long music session of bells, chimes and gongs. This music was strange but relaxing, and I would drift in and out of waking consciousness. I knew I was dreaming from time to time, but could not remember what it was about except that it felt like flying through the clouds. Later I would find that this session lasted maybe forty-five minutes to an hour.

After that, Dan would begin a longer, powerful session of seriously loud drumming and percussion. I would continue to drift in and out, sometimes dreaming, sometimes awake. Sooner or later I would feel my body tense up, then release. I had many physical sensations, some inconsequential, some painful, from tingling in my hands and feet to trembling and even occasional painful muscle contractions. Later John explained that this was my body releasing stored tension. The drumming seemed to go on and on, eventually reaching a crescendo and then it was suddenly over. We would all just lie there in the silence, and then some would start getting up and quietly moving around, until we were all awake. At that point John would send us outside for a break, and possibly we would eat the food we had brought. Then, back inside, we would share our experiences. Some people had strong dreams, visions or spirit journeys. Many of them had done this a number of times before, and were able to relate extensive stories. I was fascinated, but had no real inner experience to tell, so I just reported my physical reactions. These were taken just as seriously by John, Dan and the group, and I really felt part of it all. I enjoyed the intensity, and being there with everybody, all of us looking for a spiritual connection together.

Part 2

They called me Cat when I was a kid. Cat for Catherine, because I loved cats, and also because in modern dance class I would leap high into the air, and twist around and land as light as a cat. I can still feel how my pastel blue dance slippers would touch the floor just before my feet. I would imagine that I had silky pads on my toes to cushion them when I'd come down. I could leap higher than anyone else in the class. I loved it when they called me Cat. Even the teacher did it. Now the last thing I felt like doing was dancing.

I was in trouble again. My life was a mess. I just kept hearing that voice, "Why won't anything go right for me? If anything ever would I'd be plenty happy." So I was just trying to stay busy, hoping it would all work out. But deep down in my heart of hearts I knew it wouldn't. It never does. Bear with me, it's a little complicated how I got here.

I had been going to night school for my Bachelor's degree for seven or eight years. Getting that degree was the real goal of my life. Since I started working right out of high school, I really wanted that degree. It meant a lot more to me than getting a better job, because I really like my job. But every time the subject of education would come up, either socially or at work, I'd feel ashamed. I'd just have to clam up, hoping no one would ask me about my educational background. I was the youngest of four, and there was no money left for me to go to college. I'm not sure that was really true, but for some reason I just took it as gospel and didn't even question it. Maybe I didn't think I could make it in college. I kept living at home and got a job as a secretary in a local law office. It turned out I was more than adequate at that job and I was promoted. Several job changes and promotions later I surprisingly found myself running the administrative services for a prestigious Boston law firm. I was making lots of money, but I wanted something more meaningful. Something where I could make a difference for people. This was a big career change, but eventually I landed my current position, as the administrator for a city-wide social services provider. Now I was pretty much my own boss, and I run my own show.

Even though I felt I was set career-wise, around the time I turned forty I decided to do something about my educational background, or lack thereof. So, I researched the available programs in Boston, and settled on Metropolitan College at BU. I started the program when I was forty-one, and I graduated when I was forty-nine. That was one long haul. I was elated when I finally graduated. At first I enjoyed my new-found freedom, with time in the evenings and on the weekends to read what I wanted, spend time with my boyfriend, and do some of the things I had been telling myself I would do when it was all over.

Then I began to feel at loose ends. Suddenly I realized I had a lot of time on my hands. I was about to turn fifty, and I didn't know what I wanted anymore. I started to get the jitters, and spare time became a burden, not a pleasure. I really didn't know what I was going to do with myself.

The universe, as John calls it, intervened.

My mother had been ill for years, and around that time she took a turn for the worse. She was eighty-seven, and was a two-pack-a-day smoker for most of her adult life. She always said, "I'd rather smoke than eat," and then she would laugh about it in that throaty, hoarse voice. That really came around and bit her in the end. It was no surprise that she now had severe emphysema. It was really hard for me to see her like that, gasping for every breath and with the oxygen all the time. She couldn't even carry on a conversation, even then, and moving around under her own steam was impossible. Since I was the youngest, and still local, and the only girl, it was my responsibility to take care of her. My brothers hardly showed up at all, or called. In addition to going to the hospital every day to visit her, I had to handle all the doctors and nurses, and the insurance, and her bills and finances. It was truly exhausting. I felt if I didn't take care of her, nobody else would do it, but I was really feeling the strain.

When that medical crisis passed, she needed to enter a nursing home. In addition to her lung condition, which required continuous oxygen, she had become senile, and could no longer take care of herself. It was heartbreaking. I had to research the options, and make a choice for her. Seeing the various facilities was shocking. I did the best I could for her. Once settled, she rarely recognized me when I arrived for my daily visit. Day by day I was losing her, and I didn't want her to go. Even though we had our differences, I did love her, and I just couldn't see life ahead without her.

I began researching my mother's conditions, seeking anything that might help her. I knew I was grasping at straws, but I felt it was my duty as her daughter to find anything that could save her. So here I was again, working full time, spending evenings at the nursing home, and using every available moment to find anything that might help Mamma. I was running myself into the ground again. When I went for my annual physical, my doctor suggested that I needed an antidepressant or similar medication to slow me down, and he wanted me to follow up with a referral to a psychopharmacologist. That clinched it for me. I didn't want the drugs, but I knew two things. for sure. Number one, I was in deep trouble, and, number two, it was time to see John again.

So I called John for an appointment. I hadn't been in touch with him recently, and he was glad to hear from me, "So Catherine, what can I do to help you?"

It was a relief to hear his voice on the phone. I blurted it out, "I've got to see you, John. I'm in trouble again."

"Is it an emergency?"

"Not really."

"OK. How about next Tuesday? In the meantime, have you been meditating?"

"No."

"See if you can fit it in to your schedule. OK?"

"OK, John. I'll try, but it doesn't seem to do anything for me right now."

"Just try. I'll see you Tuesday at nine o'clock."

I was wondering if I could make it till Tuesday, almost a week away. But I did, and by the time I walked through John's office door, I was feeling a little better just from the fact of being able to talk to him again. I told him my story about Mamma, and even about my degree. He was pleased for me about that.

John said that underneath all the frenetic activity I was sad and depressed. I don't know how you can call that depression, but I guess it is. Maybe I was disappointed with my life. It was certainly true that lots of times I felt like I wasn't going anywhere, just stuck in the middle of my life. I guess I was pretty desperate by then.

The acupuncture John gave me relaxed me, but I found I couldn't sit still long enough to meditate. Too much to do. Too much to think about. So John gave me herbs to take, but I was still very depressed and couldn't snap out of it.

I had come to see John several times, and was beginning to wonder if he could really help me. We were talking about my mother's illness. I was telling him how diminished she had become. "She's really not even there anymore," I told him. "I hardly recognize her, and she never knows who I am."

"Do you think you can just let go of her?" John asked. It hit me right between the eyes. I had never actually thought of her dying. "You are so wrapped up in trying to save her, and she's already really gone," he continued.

"But it's my duty to take care of her, isn't it, John? She's not dead yet."

"That's true, Catherine, but she will need to go at some point, sooner or later. For now, you are not taking care of yourself. Look at you. You're so fatigued that you need continual stimulus just to get from one moment to the next!"

"So what should I do?" I asked him warily. I was afraid of what he was going to say next. I think I knew what was coming.

"Catherine, I think you need to do a separation with your mother. You need to give her permission to die."

"No, John!" I almost screamed at him. "What will I do without her?"

"This just shows me how overly attached to her you are," John replied gently. "Catherine, we need to work on this together."

"No, John," I refused firmly. "I won't. It's not right."

"Let me ask you a question then, Catherine. Is there ever a right time for someone to let go of a parent who is dying?"

"Well, I suppose so," I answered grudgingly.

"Do you think sometimes that the child might not know that it was the time?"

"I guess."

"How would such a child find out when it was the right time?"

"I don't know."

"That's right. However, I can see that your attachment to your mother is hurting you, and her as well. It's hurting you by draining off your energy that you need to get on with your life. Didn't you just finish complaining to me how stuck you feel? And it's holding her so that she can't easily leave. Isn't she getting ready to go?"

"You can see this?" I was shocked at the sharpness of his description. "Clearly?"

"Yes, Catherine, I can see that you are hurting yourself badly. It's time to let her go."

"I'll think about it."

"Catherine, think about it, but also feel in your heart whether I am right."

"I can't do it. John I've got to go."

"OK. Same time next week?"

"I'm not sure yet. I'll call you."

I couldn't wait to get out of there. I felt, "How dare he suggest such a thing?" And then I would think, "But he knows what he's doing. Look how he helped you before!" I was in such a dither that I really shouldn't have been driving.

A few weeks went by, and I kept postponing my next appointment with John. I knew that he would suggest the same thing, and I just didn't want to face it. However, finally I had to make the call, and went back to see him. To my surprise he didn't broach the subject, and neither did I. We just chatted for the whole time. Then he asked me, "Catherine, I'm holding a drumming seminar this Sunday, will you come?"

I was caught by surprise, and I gave myself a minute to think about it before answering, "You know, John, I was really uncomfortable the last time."

"It's entirely up to you."

Finally I agreed, "Sure, I'll come. Where and when?"

That Sunday I went to the drumming session. It was similar to the ones I had attended previously. There were about a dozen people there, and some seemed more anxious than me. As I was listening to the bells I found myself relaxing more than I had expected, and I actually fell asleep. I barely awoke as the drumming began, and then I was back in dreams and visions. I was a cat. Not sort of like a cat, but actually a cat. I realized that I was Loco, my long-haired grey cat who had died several years before. It was dark and wet. I was running down a long alley. I ran and ran forever. I couldn't get out. I was terrified, but I didn't get tired. I just kept running. There was no way out. Then I woke up and the session was over.

Afterwards, John was ecstatic. He kept saying that my dream was a vision, and it was a portal. I couldn't understand him, but he was insistent that I come to see him the next day. He said he'd make time for me. It was impossible to disagree, so I went. His pleasure was infectious, and I even found myself looking forward to talking about it some more.

But that was not what John had in mind. "Let's go back to the alley, Catherine," he insisted. "This vision is a portal, and it leads somewhere else. We need to follow it. Can you get back into the feeling of Loco running down the alley? Oh, I see, you're there already!"

And so we went. I say we, because it was entirely evident that John was there too. He didn't interfere, but I could feel him running along with me. Again I was Loco. The alley was midnight dark, and it was pouring rain. Everything was cold, wet and damp. As I ran I could see the moisture dripping from the brick walls on either side. I was afraid. More than afraid. I was filled with an unnameable fear, an unspeakable terror. I was running and running away from something immense, I knew not what. At first I had boundless energy, but as time went on I began to tire. It became harder and harder to move forward. I slowed, and then moved forward step by step only by a great act of will. I saw a point of light ahead a long way off. I kept moving, but slower and slower. Finally I reached the light, but I could move no more. I sagged down. I could not move one more step, and at that exact moment, incredibly, a wave of force lifted me up and carried me to the light, and then I was through it and somewhere else entirely.

I was at the seashore. It was dawn. The sky was just lightening, with gentle pinks and grays along the horizon, and a deep, deep blue overhead. It was warm and dry, but I could smell the delicious salt air. Waves lapped gently on the shore to my left. The sand was dry and fine under my feet, my own two feet. On my right there were dunes stretching as far as I could see, with marsh grass gently waving in the light breeze. From behind a large royal blue and white striped tent, a man dressed from head to toe in grey was walking towards me, smiling. He had charcoal grey suede boots, a dark grey suit of some coarse cloth, and a grey fedora with a long speckled feather stuck in the hatband. His goatee was salt-and-pepper against very pale skin.

"Hello, Catherine. How are you?" he asked casually.

I was taken aback. This had all happened in an instant, and I could still feel the alley, though that was fading away rapidly. "I'm OK," I stammered. "Where are we?"

"As you can plainly see, we are at the seashore. What can I do for you?"

"What do you mean? Do I get three wishes or something?" I blurted out, my face flushing with embarrassment at my rudeness.

"No," he chuckled. "But I can help you whenever you need it. All you have to do is come here and call my name."

"What's your name?"

"Call me Alejandro."

"Alejandro?"

"Yes, Alejandro."

"Whenever I need help? Like what kind of help?"

"If you need advice. Or you want company for a while. Or maybe you might want to help someone else."

"Really?"

"Just come here and call me. I will always be here waiting for you."

He began to walk away, and looked back over his shoulder. "I've always been here for you. I've just been waiting for you to come and seek me out." With that he walked down the beach back around the other side of the striped tent, and I came back to see John grinning at me.

I was so excited that I was speechless, a rarity for me. John just sat there smiling.

"That was wonderful, Catherine!" he beamed. "You did so well!"

"I did? What did I do?"

"You met one of your spirit guides, and a very nice one, too."

"Really?"

"How can you doubt it?" he chuckled. At that point I just started laughing too.

"You've let go of something, big time!" he said.

We just laughed together for a long time.

In the coming weeks John and I went back to the seashore several times, until he was sure I could do it by myself. Each time, when I would meet

Alejandro, I could feel John backing away, letting me have my time alone with the guide. During these weeks my depression began to fade, and I felt myself enjoy life again. I'm don't think I had felt that way since I was a young child. After a while John asked me the question I had so dreaded.

"Can you let go of your mother now, Catherine?"

"I think I can, John. You know she's been in a coma for several weeks."

"OK, let's call her, as you've learned."

We called Mamma.

"She's above your left shoulder, Catherine. Can you feel her? She's beautiful."

"I can't see her, but I can feel her."

"She's ready to move away now. You can talk to her if you want."

"Mamma, I so want you to be happy. I love you. It's OK for you to leave me now."

I could hardly speak from crying tears of relief and happiness.

"She's moved away now, Catherine. She was radiant with love."

"John, I'm so happy," I sobbed. I cried for a long time.

"Catherine, you did that so beautifully." He was grinning again. I started laughing, and I left his office that day the most happy I had ever been.

Back in the hospital, Mamma lingered on for another month and a half, but my relationship with her was entirely different than it had been. I would just sit with her, and sometimes I'd talk with Alejandro about her. I noticed she seemed peaceful, and one day she just drifted away. I was sad for awhile. Then I went on with my life, going about my business, and visiting the seashore and Alejandro whenever I needed help. Of course I stayed in touch with John, and we always smiled to remember that fine day in his office when we went to the beach together.

A Conversation with John Myerson on Learning to Love

This interview was conducted by Robert Greenebaum with shamanic healer John Myerson.

RG: Today we are discussing Catherine's story. How would you describe her when she first came to see you?

JM: When she sat down I could feel it. She was very, very wound up, very tense. Not that she was actually shaking in front of me, but that's what it felt like. Sometimes people are so wound up that they can't really sit still—like they are jumping. That's what she felt like to me. All she wanted to do was get up and run, instead of sitting and talking about whatever was going on with her. She was in a lot of pain. However, when I looked at her in the shamanic realms I couldn't see anything wrong with her neck and shoulders besides tightness. I might have expected to see a disc injury, or a ligament problem, or something else out of whack. There was none of that. So the cause of her pain was not physical. It was something else.

RG: You could actually sense in some way whether she had more of a physical injury than...

JM: Yes.

RG: You're saying you see that? You actually visually see that?

JM: With her I did. Sometimes I feel it, but with her I actually saw it. I looked at her spine and her shoulder, and it looked fine to me.

RG: Are you saying that you examined her physically?

JM: I didn't touch her, no. She was sitting on the couch in front of me. I never touched her.

RG: And you were sitting in your chair.

JM: Correct, I never physically touched her to examine her.

RG: Is this something that you can do under any circumstances, or is this something that you were "shown" with her?

JM: I can often do this if I choose, depending on the clarity of the connection with the person. We both know people who are medical intuitives, who can read people. I'm not sure I'd call myself a medical intuitive, although I can do part of it, obviously, especially if the connection with the person is very strong. In this case I could feel a strong connection.

RG: With her pain?

JM: Yes, I could feel her pain very strongly. And with that feeling comes an empathy—having had that pain myself! (laughs)

RG: Who hasn't had neck pain?

JM: My old football injury! So when she described the fact that she couldn't turn her head without pain shooting up into her skull—I've been there!

RG: Did you get a connection right away of what the pain was about?

JM: This poor woman was vibrating sitting here on the couch. She literally looked like she wanted to run. She would have been much more comfortable if she was running, not sitting.

RG: Running away from you.

JM: Running away from me or anyone else. We see this all the time with people who can't sit and feel their own emotions. So what they do is to literally run from it. They over-schedule themselves. They over-work. They over-do everything. That way they don't have to deal with their emotions. They just collapse, and then they wake up and do it all over again. Over the years doing that wears you down. She is a good example of that. She was all worn down. She just couldn't take it anymore.

RG: It occurs to me that you're talking about the "flight" part of "fight or flight."

JM: Yes, she was always in "flight." She was always running on adrenaline. It's hard for someone like this. Like the cartoons on TV. You are running, running, running. And behind you are your emotions, and they are running, running, running too. You have to stay ahead of them, because if you stop, they don't. They hit you.

RG: You are saying Catherine is completely disconnected from her feelings.

JM: I would agree with that. The first step is to get her to slow down, to stop, and to start feeling. The first way I did that with her was to use acupuncture. Acupuncture can release the emotional build-up. It can make her relax. And it helps her to connect with me. If she can connect to me, then she can start to connect to herself. If she can connect to herself, then she can connect to the universe.

And that is the pattern that I use. So, the first thing is to get her to connect to me. I do that by talking to her, empathizing with her, feeling her pain so she can feel that I can feel her pain; getting her to feel any type of emotion at all; using the acupuncture to relax her so she would trust me, and so she would actually be able to feel her emotions.

And then I have her meditate. Meditation is a way of learning how to change how you view the world. It is what I call a spiritual technology, in that it is training for your mind. It's like running a marathon, except we are going to use our minds instead. This is marathon training for our minds. We need to slow down. We have to get to a place where the chatter fades—all that stuff that goes on in your mind, that's the chatter. Until we can get the chatter to fade, it's hard to connect to the universe. You need to realize that you and your thoughts are not the same. One of the great discoveries of the Buddha is that if you don't attach your mind to a thought it has no power or energy. It just disappears. You learn that when a thought comes in you just don't pay attention to it. You pay attention to the breath instead. So you are going to use your breath to trick your mind away from focusing on the thought. Instead you focus on your breath.

RG: She had some difficulty doing this.

JM: Yes, everybody does. I have yet to meet anybody who finds it easy at the beginning. Some people take to it quickly, but it's not easy for anybody. And it was definitely not easy for her. She had a lot of courage to persist in doing it, even when it was scary for her. The acupuncture helps that because it releases some of the emotion.

RG: What's the relationship between the thoughts and the feelings—and the feelings associated with the thoughts? I'm referring to the fact that on the one hand she complains of the thoughts going around and around in her head, and on the other hand she has neck pain.

JM: The neck pain was a direct result of her mind being wound very, very tight. And it gets wound tight by having too many things in it. When that happens the blood flow is constricted in certain areas—in this case the neck. That's what was giving her the neck pain. This mind-body connection has been proven many times. The pain could be in the leg, in the back, in the neck—headaches, all different kinds of things. In her case it was her neck.

RG: It occurs to me that how the pain would manifest depends upon her body image of herself. For instance, if she thinks that the thoughts are in her head, and there are so many of them that she can't keep track of them all—or the same one keeps hitting her again and again, like a repetitive gong—then she's using her body image to hurt herself. So, when you are saying to her, " Watch your thoughts go by. They are not your own. They are not really even in you," you are changing her body image, as well as releasing.

JM: Yes, I agree.

RG: In the story you ask her how she is feeling. How many times did you have to ask her that before she could really feel anything?

JM: I have no idea, but it's always a lot. Once she got it, she actually looked into what I was saying. That's about all you can do, just keep after it. What I do is keep mirroring her emotions back to her. If she feels anything at all then I increase that so she can feel it even more.

RG: How do you do that?

JM: I can feel her emotions on my body, and I just increase the vibration and send it back.

RG: Do you use your own energy, or do you feel that the energy of the universe is helping you?

JM: The energy of the universe is coming through me. If I used my own energy I wouldn't last very long doing this.

RG: An analogy might be that of returning a tennis ball. You send it back to her.

JM: I send it back to her but increased—with more vibration.

RG: And her habit would be to run away from that.

JM: Right. I just wait until I feel that she is open, and I keep pushing. I push by asking her. I also push by hopefully making her feel a little bit. It can be a slow process. It's a scary thing, to feel these emotions that she possibly has never felt before.

RG: Nobody really knows why that is. It could be related to the style of the family. Or it could be related to one particular parent that she modeled. Or it could possibly be related to a past-life abuse situation. You don't know, really.

JM: Absolutely, most psychotherapy would start there with the family. Sometimes I do, but usually I try to make the connection first, and then I go back to the family. In this case it was her mother that needed work in the second part of the story. But it could have been anybody in the family that she might need to go back and separate from. Usually I start with the connection first.

RG: Her connection with herself—getting to that point.

JM: Right.

RG: That gives her the strength to do it.

JM: Right. And we're dealing with it in a different way than merely cognitive. So there is a process of analyzing, feeling, and then psychically—shamanically—letting it go.

RG: You are saying it's even beyond the experiential. Because experience is in everyday time, while being is in no-time. I've heard you mention that healing takes no-time at all. But getting to that point can be pretty time-consuming.

JM: To use another analogy of Zen—you come to a cliff. You inch closer to the cliff. And you inch, and inch, and inch. And finally you get to where you're sitting on the edge of that cliff. Healing happens when you jump. The jump corresponds to taking a step into the shamanic realms. All the inching is getting up to that place. For Catherine that was starting to feel, slowing her mind down, letting go of the thoughts. Jumping was opening herself up to the universe and getting to a place where she could really feel.

RG: Somehow you have to figure out a different strategy for each person to get them to the cliff, because each one is different. The cliff might be the same, but the person is different.

JM: Absolutely! Shamans all over the world use anything they possibly can to get people to that place. Anything. You read about shamans who trick them, who laugh at them, who make themselves like clowns, who make them climb mountains. Anything they can get you to do is fine, as long as it gets you to jump. That's the trick at being good at what I do. It's getting people to that place—and then being there for them when they do jump. With Catherine it was the connection with her. It was letting her know that I was there for her. It was letting her know that I cared for her. It was letting her know that someone could share what she was feeling. And that was important to her. Everybody will be different.

RG: It seems that Catherine—and most people—would have to take a few smaller leaps before taking the "Big One." Even just coming to see you is one of those small steps.

JM: There are all kinds of leaps in the story, if you look at it. Coming in the door, having acupuncture, sitting down and meditating at all, then continuing with the meditation, and then calling the souls—those are all epiphanies if you ask me. Probably the biggest epiphany was in Part 2 in the drumming session when she had the vision.

RG: What about your teaching her to call the souls?

JM: Yes, that was a big one, but I think when she and I reviewed the vision, and went down the tunnel—which was the alley—and came out on the beach, that was when she jumped off the cliff. That's the big cliff! The others were little cliffs.

RG: She actually went through other tunnels, too. If you start right with the beginning, the pain itself is one of those tunnels.

JM: Right. And tunnels are always transformative.

RG: And just being in the room with you is another one.

JM: Correct. And sitting here in the room with me is not always the easiest thing to do, because the energy here is very strong. It vibrates a lot, and it can be very scary, even though I try to make it safe. There's no confrontation, but it's just scary because of the energy, and also because of what I'm asking them to do. And to keep coming back every week is also facing a tunnel every time. For instance, Catherine had to drive an hour to get here. That's facing a tunnel right there, every single time! (laughs) But the tunnels, as I said, are always transformative. You come out the other side and something always has changed.

RG: And it's changed to the point where actually you can't go back to where you were. Time has moved on. You've moved on. The landscape has changed, and it's just different.

JM: Right. I had a patient yesterday who has this elaborate scenery that he goes through to get to get to his tunnels and places. And he was trying to hold onto it all. So every time he'd meditate, he'd start from where he began and go through all this scenery. It was taking him hours. He couldn't keep doing it. I asked him, "Why are you holding onto this scenery?" (laughs) The scenery is meaningless. It's where you get to that's important. You can start from there each time. You don't have to start all the way back at the beginning again.

RG: Actually, if you hold onto it you're stuck in the tunnel—forever. Let's talk a little bit about your teaching method of connecting to the souls. We have already covered the terminology of "souls," "spirits," "angels"—there are a lot of different ways that people have tried to describe this over the ages *(see page 59, ed.)*. I'd just like to indicate that your way of describing it is "souls." But this is something which actually exists. This is a connection that is actually real.

JM: Yes, and it doesn't matter to me what words you use. People call them "angels," "spirits," "guides" —it doesn't matter to me. The term that I was taught was "souls." The form of shamanism I learned is ancestor worship. It literally is about souls. That's what they're talking about. They're actually talking about people who are dead, who have left this world, and who are in another world. And they (the shamans) are connecting to the soul of that person. That's what my teacher would do. She had certain specific people who she either knew, and now were dead, or people who were generally known. We're not talking about mythological ones, and we're not talking about the Archangel Michael—but actual people who were here, and now were gone. So that's the system where it comes from. But some people relate to that, and some people don't. In the culture here in America it depends on their upbringing. Catherine came from a Roman Catholic background, so the idea of souls is not that strange, but "angels" sounds better to her. Whatever she wanted—the word is unimportant. But I would agree with you. They are real. They are not something I create in my mind. They are real. I connect to them. They exist. There is certain energy exchanged, and things happen.

RG: There's a big question involved here, about whether we—living people—are bodies with souls, or souls with bodies, or spirits with bodies. And vice versa, whether the "souls" are the spirits of dead people, or whether they pre-existed the "living" people. There's a continuum here that's being connected with in some way, as opposed to...

JM: As a shamanic healer, it doesn't matter to me. I'll use whatever lexicon you want. If you want it one way, that's fine with me. If you want it the other way that's fine with me. All that matters to me is that we make the connection, and we travel to the realms. That's all that matters to me. How we get there, I don't care.

RG: It doesn't matter to me either. What I'm trying to indicate is that just as people can say, "Well, this is real life," what is often called "the other world" is also "real life." And this is a method of connecting with that part of "real life."

JM: I absolutely agree with you. I couldn't agree with you more.

RG: How do you teach her to make this connection?

JM: I give her the "Calling the Souls" prayer. The words are not important. They are words that were given to me by my teacher. But to me it is a Dharma transmission. Dharma is a sanskrit word for the teachings of the Buddha. For example, in Zen Buddhism, where I trained, you meet with your teacher, one-on-one, and you get certain connections and information from that teacher. The connection and information you get is called a Dharma transmission. You get energy from your teacher which was received from his or her teacher all the way back to the Buddha. So, in essence, you are getting the teaching of the Buddha passed down through generations. And that's how I feel this prayer works. I give it to you. I have you write it down. And as you are doing it I connect with you and give you a transmission. I give you energy. I give you power. I give you something that's growing through you, that allows you to open a door into those other realms. You still have to step through it. But it allows you to open the door. If you were to give the prayer to somebody else it would have no power. It's because I give it to you that it works. If you were to train and do the work too, then you could give it to other people. It's not secret. It's just a power transmission. So that's what I do. When I do that with people they can feel it. The energy in the room changes. That's what I do with Catherine. I help her to open the door—by using the prayer, by using her mind, by using the power that was available to her. But it still took her time to be able to step through it. It does open the door. That's the key. But then you have your own fears, and projections, and all kinds of things that stand in the way of actually going through the door.

RG: It sounds like the Dharma transmission is teaching by example, but more than that, it is actually giving the person the ability.

JM: It's an energy transfer, and it's actually me giving you something energetically—me giving you something in another realm. I actually feel that I am giving you something.

RG: And, once again, this is not your personal energy necessarily.

JM: No. What I do is to open up to the same energy that my teacher gave me, it passes through me to you, and now it's yours. All I'm doing is passing something on. This is not unique to me. It's something that I give you through me, from the universe.

RG: And there is love connected with this.

JM: It all relates to love. That's the thing that opens the door. It's the heart chakra connection. Love is in the heart chakra, the heart, the chest. Once that connection is made then the love can flow. It comes through me, from the universe, through my heart, to you. It's directed by my mind, but it flows through me from my heart into you—into your heart.

RG: I imagine you wait until the person is ready before you try this.

JM: Yes.

RG: Sometimes are they not ready?

JM: Yes. And if they aren't ready, it doesn't work. Nothing happens. I send the energy out to you, and it doesn't go anywhere. The door stays closed. I can knock on the door all I want, but until the door is open I can't give it to you. Usually that doesn't happen because I wait until the door opens before I give it to you.

RG: In terms of training somebody—because it sounds like training—

JM: This is a training.

RG: —you would just connect to them on a person-to-person basis first. And when they can do that reliably, then you would move on from there and try something more intense—or a higher vibration—or however you would describe it.

JM: Right. Let's say Catherine came in for the neck pain, and she got better. Her neck pain went away, and that was the extent of it for her. If she didn't want to do anything else, I wouldn't have gone on with her. I would just have said, "I'm glad your neck is feeling better. Good luck to you. Maybe do some yoga to relax, or do whatever other kind of stress reduction. Keep up with the meditation. If you have problems give me a call." That would be it. But I could tell from the connection of love with her, and the energy that was exchanged between us, that she wanted to go on. And so I went on with her.

RG: I want to stop for a second. When you say "she," it's really her soul, her spirit, that wants to come out.

JM: Very good point.

RG: So then you know she's ready.

JM: I know she's ready because I can connect to her heart. I knock on the door and it's wide open. It says, "Help me. Show me more. I want to go on."

RG: Then, after she receives the prayer, the Dharma transmission, she has to go and practice it by herself.

JM: She says the prayer over and over again, and that opens the door for her. Then she meditates and sees what happens. Sometimes it's hard for people to do that, so I have them do it for other people. It's easier for her to open her heart and send others love than it is to open her heart and be in love herself. So, as an intermediate step, and a way for her to open up her own heart, I have her send love to others—people who are sick or injured. In that way she has to open her heart up, and let the energy of the universe come through her into another person. But either way, her heart is open, and that's the key.

RG: And she starts being imbued with that love, and she changes.

JM: And the more she does it, the more she changes.

RG: John, it's interesting what you're saying, because most people would think that you'd have to learn to do it for yourself first, and than you could help other people. It would be a higher skill to help other people—but actually it's a higher skill to just be who you are.

JM: I absolutely agree with that. It's much more difficult than helping people.

RG: Interesting.

JM: It is interesting. And you see people all the time who are caregivers who get sick because they are giving, giving, giving all the time, and can't receive. You have to be able to do both. But I would say that it's much harder to receive than to give.

RG: Is that because of the requirement that you have to connect with your feelings to do it?

JM: Yes, and the fact that you have to be able to accept the love, which means that you are worthy of the love. That means that you're accepting who you are, which is not always an easy thing to do. There are fears, and pain and anger, and all kinds of other things that are mixed in there, and have to be worked out before you can actually accept the love. It can be a long process.

RG: The other thing that Catherine discusses is the drumming seminar. Now, how does this whole process relate to the drumming seminar? It must be the same process that you are using.

JM: It's exactly the same process. The only difference with the drumming seminar is that the energy is more intense. In order to get to the cliff and jump off, you need a certain amount of energy. Sometimes people don't have the energy themselves, either because they're weak, or the fear is in the way—usually the fear. It's an emotion that gets in the way and is keeping them from doing that. So, what shamans have always used are techniques, ways of raising the energy of a person—the vibrational energy. The higher the vibrational energy the more chance you have of going into these other realms. In the seminars I use acupuncture to lower the energy of the sensory barrier—in other words it makes it easier to go from this reality to the other reality. And I use Tibetan bells and tone bowls and African drums. I have a wonderful master percussionist, Dan Schwartz, who conducts these drumming sessions with me. His music provides more energy and higher vibration levels.

And I create a safe environment for people. Much like I do one-on-one in a Dharma transmission, I transmit that energy to the group of participants. I can't control where each person is going, but I can open the door for them and give them energy. That's why this was successful with Catherine. In this situation she had the vision, she was in the tunnel as the cat, but she didn't get through it. That's why it was so important for me to see her the next day, so I could get her through the tunnel while she was still in the tunnel—while she still had the memory of where she was, while the energy and the power of her vision was still there.

RG: When she went to the first few of these drumming sessions, she didn't really have any visionary shamanic experiences at all.

JM: Right. But with these drumming seminars, whether you are aware of it or not, something is happening. She was just not aware of it. Her fear was such that she couldn't let herself see what was going on, but something definitely was happening. If you go to one of these, you don't just fall asleep. There is too much energy going on. There are just too many things happening. Whether you are aware, actually cognitively aware to see what's happening or not, something is still happening. This last one she went to she actually relaxed enough, she was open enough, and her fear was lessened enough, that she could see the tunnel.

RG: All her experiences with her mother may have worn her down, to the point where she was softened up. When she came back to you she was too wound up again for your treatments to be successful, and she was not able to meditate at that point in her life. But she was going through some serious emotional situations with her mother.

JM: And the reason I had her do the drumming seminar is because it is deeper. I realized that the stuff she had in the beginning was more superficial. Neck pain is superficial, as opposed to depression, anxiety, and fear. That's a little deeper. I realized that the kind of technique I had used before wasn't going to work. I needed to do something deeper with her, and she wasn't letting me connect with her. So I thought of the drumming session as being stronger. That worked. And, as you can see, the separation with her mother was a sort of by-product of all this. In most psychotherapy we sit and analyze her relationship with her mother. That's not what we were doing. We were dealing with her, and her ability to let go and jump off the cliff, and connect, and love. And when she was able to do that she was able to love her mother, and could let her go. Again, it's an example that healing happens in an instant. She could let her mother go in an instant. But it took a long time to get there.

RG: What about her vision that she had with you in your office? After she got through the alley as the cat, then she suddenly came out on the beach. There's a major change there. What changed?

JM: That's coming out of the tunnel. The tunnel is the dark place of fear. And she got right up to the edge of the cliff—that's the light that she could see at the end of the tunnel. And then she jumped. In this case I was with her, so I gently pushed, but I knew where we were going, I'd been there before.

RG: So when she feels that wave, that's actually you helping her when she takes the leap.

JM: Yes. But she leapt. I didn't kick her over the edge. She jumped. That was her doing. She brought herself there and she did it.

RG: In her vision, though, she could hardly crawl up to the light.

JM: Absolutely, some people crawl, and they scrape, and they go by tooth and nail, and it's bloody. It's not easy.

RG: You're actually going through all this with her, so you know when it's the right time to help.

JM: I've done this many, many times, not only for myself, but for other people, so I know where she is, and what's going on, and what she's feeling.

RG: Just to go back, she's running through the alley, and she feels all this pressure. She doesn't know what she's running from, and feels the pressure and the darkness. From what you were describing at the beginning of the interview that's really mostly her feelings.

JM: Her fear.

RG: Her fear of her feelings.

JM: Right. It could be any of the feelings for sure. In general it's the fear that makes her run.

RG: So the whole situation of her as the cat in the alley, in the dark and the rain, and running from an unnameable adversary—that's all fear, you are saying.

JM: Correct.

RG: That is a visionary experience of her fear.

JM: Now the cat is also interesting. She becomes a cat. The cat is one of her power animals. She didn't know that at this point in time, because she hadn't visited her power animals yet. But, like spirit guides, people also have animals that they are attracted to. In this case it's a cat. Now, she happens to be a cat lover anyway, so she takes the physical form of her cat, now dead. So the cat's soul is there too. The soul of the cat comes to help her, in his form, go through the tunnel. That's significant also to me.

RG: You're saying that the cat can be considered a spirit helper.

JM: Absolutely. So she has two of them in this experience. One is the person that she meets, and the other is the cat. The soul of the cat helps her travel.

RG: In the vision, she comes to the beach, and she meets Alejandro. Who's Alejandro? Do we know?

JM: I don't know. I never found out. You can find out, though. My teacher used to find out, for instance, who Alejandro was. Usually they are ancestors from "the way-back." Some of them are ancestors like grandmothers, grandfathers, great-grandmothers. It felt to me like Alejandro was not someone immediate, but from generations ago. I don't ask, because it doesn't matter to me. If it's an immediate thing then you usually recognize them. If it's peaceful, if it's loving, if it's to her benefit, then it doesn't matter to me. At that point I fade. We're on the beach. I see him. I check out if it's OK. If everything feels good, I stay away. (laughs) This is now her thing.

RG: You've brought her there.

JM: Yes.

RG: You accompany her.

JM: Correct.

RG: You accompany her as a traditional psychopomp.

JM: Yes, I just go out there with her. It's all safe. You know, I have come to these places, when it wasn't safe. For instance, whatever it was, she wasn't attracting the right energy, so then I have to get her back out of there to protect her. I've done that before, where I have to protect the person, and send the other person away, or immediately get out of there. But, that's rare. In this situation, it was loving, and peaceful, and it felt really good, and so I didn't worry about it. And at that point I fade into the background, and I just watch from a distance. It's now up to her. The key there is that she felt safe. And the beach is from her own imagination. It's her own place. Somewhere along the line the beach must have been a safe place for her. So, she went to this beach that was safe and secure.

RG: You wouldn't necessarily go to a beach, or a field. You could go anywhere.

JM: Anywhere.

RG: When you leap, you go somewhere, but it could be anywhere.

JM: It could be anywhere. Usually it's a place that you've been to on the earth. I have leapt and been on the Moon. (laughs)

RG: That's a traditional shamanic journey.

JM: No question. Usually it's a place that feels good. A lot of times your spirit guides will exist in these places for you. Alejandro was on the beach for her. Other ones will be in a field, or on a mountain, or in a stream, or a lake. And they are always there. That's how you meet them. You go to that place. And, if you notice, we spent the next few weeks going back to that place over, and over, and over again. So she knew the path in the spirit world to that place. Once she knew the path to that place, then my job is done. The guide will then teach her whatever it is that she needs to know.

RG: She mentions that you would take her there and then disappear.

JM: Right. It's not my thing. It's her thing. It's not my game, it's hers. And whatever transpires between her and her teacher, is between her and her teacher. To me it's a thing of power, and beauty, and love.

RG: Aren't you her teacher?

JM: In this realm, I'm her teacher. But I become more her compatriot than her teacher at that point. I'm there to help defend her, help protect her. I'm there to help her when she gets into new areas, as to who she is, and where she's going, and help her with techniques if she needs new techniques. But the teaching that happens on a psychic level happens with her and her guide.

RG: All during this time she's dealing with her mother's dying process. At some point you felt her mother was there with her, or you asked her mother to come. What happened with that?

JM: Well, I could see her mother sitting over her left shoulder—literally.

RG: Was this every time?

JM: When Catherine came back the second time—in Part 2 I could see her mother.

RG: Once again you waited until she was able to deal with that before you decided to address the issue?

JM: Yes, absolutely. I tried to address it from the beginning by having her do a separation with her mother, and she couldn't do it, so I backed right off, and tried to get her to a place where she could. And if that hadn't worked I would have backed off again and tried something else. I would have kept trying whatever it is that came to my mind to try, until I got her to a place where she could let go.

RG: That's a lot of patience on your part.

JM: That's what healing is all about, patience. (laughs)

RG: Together you call her mother, the two of you. Then she talks to her mother. In the story you tell her that she can talk to her mother if she wants. Then she does. At that point it's from her heart—because now she has one. What happened?

JM: She couldn't see it, but I could see her mother moving away, and moving off to the light, this great light, way off in the distance, and she's moving away. So, at the end she wasn't there anymore. When I called on her mother, she wasn't there. There was literally nothing there. At that point I know that Catherine had separated from her mother, and when it was her mother's time to go, she would go.

RG: Catherine actually had done a separation right then and there with her mother.

JM: Correct. Well, I did it.

RG: You did the separation, but she experienced it?

JM: Well, what happens is that I can do a separation any time. But I don't like it to be wrenching, because I only do that in cases of emergency, where I have to protect someone. I want it to be a thing of beauty and love, a thing that Catherine feels she took part in, and that is healing. To do that she has to let her mother go with love. This whole process was to get her to a place where she could turn and tell her mother, "I love you. All is peace between us. You need to go." At that point I helped her go.

RG: Just like you helped Catherine make the leap, you helped her mother make the leap too.

JM: She knows the way. The souls know that the light is to go to, and the bonds connecting her are now broken.

RG: Dissolved.

JM: Yes. They're not there anymore and she is free to go. And she moves off that way.

RG: From the point of view of the vibrations that you were talking about, in the vision, where Catherine is with Alejandro, she now is in a situation with very high vibration. She brings that back with her from the shamanic realm to this realm. She deals with this issue now inter-personally between herself and her mother in this life, and then once again, back in the shamanic realm the bonds are dissolved.

JM: Right, and as you said before, once she's made that leap she's not the same anymore. Her energy vibrations are different than they were before.

RG: And all this is done from the point of view of love.

JM: It's all love, and, when it happens and you see it, it is beautiful. Catherine is radiating love, and her mother is radiating light. She moves off and it's just a moment of beauty and peace. For me, watching it happen is a beautiful scene. Very, very beautiful.

Chapter 2

Transition &
Transformation

Alethea

I was standing at the bottom of the stairs, shivering wildly with fear. The light was so dim that I could only make out the bottom four or five steps. The heavy, warm air pressed against me from all sides, making it almost impossible to breathe. Doom and dread emanated from the very walls like a heavy lavender mist. Standing in the foyer of my grandmother's dark Victorian house, I could feel her presence. But I could not see her, and she was silent. I needed to climb those creaky old stairs, yet I could not move a muscle.

I awoke covered in a cold sweat, feeling sick and nauseous. The clammy sheets clung to my body. This was the nightmare that I had had every night for as long as I could remember. I knew I needed help. I felt that I could not go on like this much longer, but I didn't know what to do.

The next morning I was groggy and disoriented as usual. I couldn't remember the last time I had slept all night without having the dream. Ever? That was a Wednesday, and I was going to have lunch with Donna, my best friend. I left work a little early, and met her at the cozy neighborhood restaurant we called "our place." Even though I had known Donna for over ten years, I had never told her, or anyone else, about my dream. But I was at my wit's end, and I blurted out my story.

Donna was shocked, probably more at the fact that I hadn't mentioned my problem before, than at the story of the dream. How could she know how terrified I really was, anyway? Once she knew I needed help, Donna called some of her other friends, and the next day she called me at work with the names of two highly recommended therapists.

As frightened as I was from my dreams, I was more frightened of calling a therapist, and then having to go through with telling my story again. But that night I had the dream again, and I felt even worse the next morning. Early that afternoon I made the calls, and left messages on both answering machines.

It took me until the next afternoon to speak with Joyce, the first therapist. I had decided to try her first, since I thought I might feel more comfortable with a woman. I took my heart in my hands, and told Joyce my story. She offered to set up an appointment, but I didn't get the feeling that she was really interested in my situation. In fact, she was quite noncommittal, and, I suppose, very professional and distant. I was less than encouraged at really getting any help through therapy, and I gave it up for that day.

The next morning I was feeling bad again, and decided to try the second therapist, John. I was lucky, and got through to John between patients. Once again I told my story, not really expecting too much help. To my surprise John immediately began to talk to me, telling me he would be able to help me. He said, "What you are feeling is real. You are not crazy. You are not going out of your mind. And I can help you." He listened to me, and I felt that he was really there for me. To my surprise I started calming down just from talking to him. I felt a real connection with him right away. At that point I felt I didn't need any more reassurances, and I made an appointment to see John the following week.

When the day for my appointment came, I could hardly think of anything else. I kept asking myself over and over, "Will he really be able to help me?" I hoped we would get along as well in person as we had on the phone. I got into my car to go to his office, and, as I closed the door, I started shaking again, and the tears came. "Please, please let this be over," I said to myself, with clenched teeth. I gripped the steering wheel firmly with both hands. I had to let myself calm down a little before I could pull into traffic.

When I met John, I again had a strong sense of connection. I was still frightened, but maybe without the edge of absolute terror that I had had in the car. To my surprise, he was not too interested in my history, but started immediately asking about the nightmares. He was genuinely interested in my answers, and completely attentive. While I was talking about my dream, I had the peculiar sensation that he understood my terror perfectly. We talked for an hour, and then he asked, "Shall we meet again next week?" I had to decide whether to come back, and I realized how much calmer I had become talking with him. I made another appointment for the following week. John said he would be working with me every morning. I didn't understand what he meant, but it felt good that he cared enough to think about me. I left with a feeling of being uplifted for the first time in a very long while.

My second appointment with John was a little easier. I knew how to get to his building, and I knew what to expect when he called me in to his office. He asked me how I was, and we began talking about my nightmare again. John said, "You know, Alethea, your grandmother's house in your dream is real, and there is some reason you keep going back there every night. I'd like to go there with you." Well, I was certainly shocked. I mean, how can somebody go into another person's dream? I asked John, "What do you mean, exactly? You're scaring me, John."

John explained, "Alethea, what we will do is talk about your dream together. As we are talking, I will feel what you are feeling, and I will help you." I didn't know what to do, and I told John. He said, "Don't worry, all you have to do is sit right where you are, relax, close your eyes, and talk about your dream." I thought, "I came here for help, and he is saying this will help." Another voice said, "I don't think this will do any good, how can just talking together accomplish anything?" Finally, I overcame my fears, looking at John as he smiled, and agreed to try it. I closed my eyes and thought about the nightmare. And I told John,

I am standing at the bottom of the stairs, shivering wildly with fear. The light is so dim that I can only make out the bottom four or five steps. The heavy, warm air presses against me from all sides, making it almost impossible to breathe. Doom and dread emanate from the very walls like a heavy lavender mist. Standing in the foyer of my grandmother's dark Victorian house, I can feel her presence. But I cannot see her, and she is silent. I need to climb those creaky old stairs, yet I cannot move a muscle. Someone is holding my hand, and talking to me.

I was so startled that I opened my eyes and made a little gasp. John opened his eyes and smiled at me. He asked me what happened, and I told him. He just laughed, said we were making progress already, and asked me when would I like to come back. Again he said, "I will be working with you during the week. If anything else changes, don't be afraid. Call me if you need help." And then he added, "Alethea, see if you can spend a few minutes each day thinking like this about your dream." As I walked out to my car, I noticed how fast the clouds were blowing across the sky.

During the rest of that week I thought about my nightmare for a few minutes each day. I wasn't sure it was doing any good, but I trusted John, and he had said to try it, so I did. I did notice that, even though I still had the nightmare, that I was a little calmer than usual during the day. At night it was the same old terror.

When I returned to John's office the following week, he greeted me with a big smile and asked how I was doing. I replied that I was still having the nightmare, but that I felt better knowing that he was helping me. Again John said, "Alethea, tell me about your nightmare again." So I did. While I was telling John about my dream, I had the strange sensation that, even though I was awake, that I was there in the foyer of the mansion too. And, after a while, I realized that John was there again too. He was holding my hand and talking to me. "Alethea," he said, "See if you can take a step forward, towards the stairs." I couldn't move, but I thought, "John says to take a step towards the stairs."

We stayed like that a long time. But this was something new for me. In my dream, I was frozen to the spot, but I was thinking about moving. A little piece of the terror moved aside for an instant now and then, and I could think of what I wanted to do. John was there, holding my hand, and talking to me through it all. And then it was time to leave.

I came back each week for four or five weeks, and we went into my nightmare together and stood at the bottom of the stairs. I thought about climbing the stairs, but could not move. The terrible lavender mist got heavier and heavier, and clung to me. John was right there with me every moment, but I was getting very frustrated and jumpy. I asked him, "Are we getting anywhere?" He answered, "Alethea, don't worry, this is just something you have to go through to get on with your life. We will do it together." And he grinned at me in that way he has. I left, and each day I continued to sit down and think about the nightmare for a few minutes. John had said that he was still "working with me" every morning as well.

The next time I saw John, he welcomed me in to his office with a big laugh. We got right down to it, and went into the mansion. This time the mist grew heavier than I had ever felt. I was almost crushed with terror, but somehow I held on. I could feel John holding my hand:

I am standing at the bottom of the stairs, shivering wildly with fear. The light is so dim that I can only make out the bottom four or five steps. The heavy, warm air presses against me from all sides, making it almost impossible to breathe. Doom and dread emanate from the very walls like a heavy lavender mist. Standing in the foyer of my Grandmother's dark Victorian house, I can feel her presence. But I cannot see her, and she is silent. I need to climb those creaky old stairs, yet I cannot move a muscle. John is holding my hand, and talking to me, saying, "Alethea, try to take a step toward the stairs. I can feel how scared you are, but we can handle it together. Just take a step."

At that point I managed to move. I stepped forward with my right foot, and suddenly we were on the stairs. I could hardly stand the pressure of the lavender mist around me. With each step higher, the pressure, and the terror, increased until I could hardly keep from screaming and running back down. But somehow I managed to take another step, and another. All at once, we were on the landing, halfway to the top. The stairs turned, and I managed to look up, and that's when I saw the top step as it reached the dark second floor hallway. And then we were back in John's office, and it was daytime again. I started crying right away, and John said, "Alethea, everything is fine. You did great." And he smiled again.

During that week I had a feeling of setting down a great burden. I felt like crying often, but it was the good kind of crying, a relief. I continued to spend a few minutes each day thinking about my dream, and I noticed that I was thinking a lot about what was on the second floor, at the top of the stairs. On Wednesday I had lunch with Donna again, at "our place", and she remarked to me, "Oh Alethea, I have never seen you so happy!" I didn't know what to say, I just started crying again.

Still, the nightmare haunted me. And as I returned to John's office again, I found myself wishing that this was all behind me. After greeting me with his usual laugh, John said, "Alethea, today I would like to teach you a prayer to say each day, before you think about your dream." He told me the prayer, one line at a time, and I wrote it down on the back of a flyer he gave me. Then he said, "Can you feel anything different than a few minutes ago, before we said the prayer?" I could feel a tingling on my skin, and the air seemed to crackle with static electricity. I said so, and John remarked, "They are here with us, Alethea, to help us. To help you." A little startled, and feeling anxious, I asked, "What do you mean, John? Who's here?" He said, "The souls that are meant to protect and heal you are here, you have called them, and when they are called they must come." I started feeling scared, but then I realized that I felt warm and comfortable, and cared about.

After a few minutes John asked me to go to the landing on the stairs with him. Immediately we were in the mansion, in the terror, in the heavy lavender mist. The mist grew heavier and heavier, pressing in from all sides. John urged me to climb up to the second floor hallway. I gripped the bannister, and began to climb the steps again. With a sharp jolt I came down on the second floor, still surrounded by the heavy mist.

The second floor hallway was open to the stairs on one side, with a balustrade. The bedrooms had doors along the other three sides. The pressure and terror was almost intolerable. This was no place to linger, and there was no way I was going back down those stairs. John and I bent our heads into the mist and walked step by step towards the only bedroom door that was slightly open. A dim light came from the door opening, slightly brighter than the surrounding gloom. Suddenly we were inside.

As soon as we entered the room, the entire atmosphere changed. The pressure and fear that had resisted us all the way from the bottom of the stairs was gone. In its place was a sullen darkness that was no less terrify-ing. I noticed a few pieces of furniture along the walls. John said, "Alethea, walk across the room." I started to walk, and then immediately we were free, out in a bright golden landscape.

The warm fields stretched ahead of us, under a scintillating blue sky. There was an enormous feeling of love and belonging, there in the fields. We were up on a hill, and a road went down towards a river. We walked along the road together. We went down, and then, as I came over the last rise before the river, I saw a log cabin on the near bank. There was a beautiful woman wearing a print cotton shirtwaist dress sitting in a rocking chair on the porch. She was smiling at me, and I felt a feeling of welcoming from her. I let go of John's hand and walked up to the woman. She stood up and came towards me, still smiling warmly.

"Alethea," she said to me in her musical voice, "I have been waiting for you. I am so glad you came, sit down with me." I was a little wary, but she was so charming, I just felt right at home, and so I sat down with her. She said, "Althea, you won't be frightened any more. And your nightmare will never return. I am your spirit master, and now that you have found me, you can come and talk to me anytime you wish. I will always be here for you." And she told me her name, and said I could call her anytime.

Then we were back in John's office, and he was smiling at me again, looking sort of expectant. I told him what happened, and he said, "You did it, Alethea. I don't think you are going to have any more nightmares after this." I left there feeling really exhilarated for the first time in a long while.

As I look back on that day, I realize that it was a major turning point in my life. I started sleeping all night, and I became much more energetic and active. I still visit that cabin on the river whenever I need help.

A Conversation with John Myerson on Transition and Transformation

This interview was conducted by Robert Greenebaum with shamanic healer John Myerson.

RG: John, Alethea goes through a succession of doors in her story. In her dream—she goes through the door to the house into the foyer. Somehow she got in there—because it's a house. When you get to the top of the stairs, she goes though the bedroom door, and then you go out the window or through the wall to the field. There are a whole series of doors. What are these doors?

JM: We all go through emotional or spiritual blockages to get to other places. For example, someone wants to climb a tree, but he gets to the first branch of the tree and he freezes. So, he has a block there. He has a gateway, a doorway, he has to go through, before he can get to the next branch of the tree. In that case it's fear. Some people would have such a block doing anything physical like that. And in the shamanic sense they are roadblocks that lead us into another place. So, one would experience these things, and many times they're experienced as tunnels. A tunnel can take any form at all. It can be a tunnel in the ground that you go into. It could be a cave. It could be a stairwell. And with Alethea, there's the tunnel starting at the doorway of the house. And then it becomes the stairway. Then it becomes the dark room. I could just sense that it was a tunnel. It was a feeling of energy that needs to be gone through.

RG: It's enclosed. You are trapped in the tunnel. You can go on—that's about your only choice.

JM: And you can get stuck in them, like Alethea was stuck for weeks in the tunnel. Stanislov Grof or Wilhelm Reich, Freud's disciple, were into "birth canals." They likened these tunnels to a rebirthing experience. In other words there's that whole Rebirthing movement, and Grof has his holotropic breathwork movement. They liken the tunnel to being reborn—re-experiencing your birth.

RG: Anthropological work related to aboriginal shamans describes the transforming experience of going through the tunnel as a universal experience all over the world in many different societies.

JM: Absolutely. And if you read Joseph Campbell, the famous mythologist, he has shown that in many different societies. It doesn't matter—the Inuit would have a tunnel in the ice, Jung had a stairway because he lived in Switzerland, other people use caves. I've seen people use rabbit holes, or burrows under a tree. It really doesn't matter. Anything that is dark and enclosed will work. And houses work.

RG: The experience for the person is actually the process of transforming. It's very unpleasant for them. The traditional shamanic experience is one of dismemberment.

JM: That's what they call it. It's like dying. That's why Grof and Reich called it rebirthing. You die and are reborn. And that's a very common theme in shamanic lore—for people to die and get reborn.

RG: Alethea's visionary experience of her grandmother's house is the fear itself.

JM: This wasn't actually her grandmother's house. It was, in the beginning. But as soon as she started being in it with everything, the grandmother disappeared, and the house disappeared. And it wasn't her grandmother's house. So I don't know why it's "her grand-mother's house."

RG: Well, it's called her grandmother's house in the story.

JM: No, I'm saying, for her, I'm not sure what the relationship was. I didn't really care, because she had no fear of her grandmother. This wasn't a fearful place, and when she stood outside and then walked in, it was her grandmother's house. But as soon as she got in it wasn't. Somehow her grandmother seemed to disappear anyway.

RG: My opinion and my own experience is that, for instance, you have a fear in what we call normal waking reality, but when you go into the shamanic realm it can be anything. Her fear could be embodied as the house and the stairway—that is her fear. Or, for somebody else it could be a palm tree, or anything. So, I'm curious whether you can recall other patients whose specific emotion was embodied as an object?

JM: That becomes the tunnel. They all turn into a tunnel. Whatever the fear is becomes a tunnel. And that's why I like people to sit and look and follow it. So, in other words, the process for everybody is that you feel the fear—and you go towards it. You don't go away from it. The more you run, the stronger it gets. So, it's like *St. George and the Dragon*. You've got to turn and face the dragon.

RG: Which means going through the tunnel...

JM: Which means you have to look at the tunnel, and then you've got to go into the tunnel. So, I didn't know what we were really getting into in this. All I knew is that you had to keep pushing against it. You had to keep going against the fear. And by experience, I know that eventually it comes out somewhere else. Where it was going to come out I had no idea. But I knew it would.

RG: We were talking a moment ago about the shamanic initiation, the dis-memberment—the tradition of the initiation—and I know that you have a personal experience of going through a tunnel inside a big tree at one point during your apprenticeship. Could you describe that experience?

JM: Well, there are two different tree stories. The first time I went through the tunnel it was a lot like Alethea's experience, but I did this in a trance. This was shamanic journeying accompanied with drums. What would happen is that I would get caught in the tunnel. So, I would start my journey, and I would go into this dark place. I would be surrounded by the tunnel, and it would get dark and condensed and enclosed. I felt like I was suffocating. I could feel myself moving, but I wasn't going anywhere. I was surrounded by dark. It was very painful physically, like I was being crushed. But the fear was too much and I could never get through it.

I kept getting stuck in the darkness. I would come out of the journey with anger, rage, or fear. I would be traveling along and then something out of the darkness of the tunnel would always scare me and send me back. I would say it took about eight or ten tries before one day I just decided I wasn't going to back down anymore. And I was —POOF!— right out of the tunnel. All of a sudden I popped out, and I was in this big field. I felt like I had come out from a tree into this big, big field. It was nice and golden and warm. In front of me in this field was this huge tree. It was a maple tree, rounded, looking perfect in an early Fall light. The leaves hadn't turned. It was still green, but it was that golden color you get in the Fall. The grass was not green. It was field grass, swaying in the breeze. Everything was very golden, and the tree was light green—the leaves were light green and the tree was very dark. So that was my first experience of passing through the tunnel. The feeling was of light and love, and openness and transformation. The fear was all totally gone. And I just walked towards the tree. The tree felt like a grandfather. It felt like it was welcoming me in. It was warm and embracing. I just kept walking towards it, until I felt I was embraced by the energy of the tree. The tree embraced me with its energy. It called out to me and touched me with golden lines of energy that passed from the tree to me. I had never had such a feeling of love and total acceptance. And that was the experience. I just stayed there with that tree. Since that time I never have had trouble going through the tunnel again.

So that was the first time I actually got through the tunnel. Much like Alethea's tunnel the first time she actually made it all the way up the stairs and out from the room into her field. They don't always go into fields. It's just that one had to do with me, and the other with her.

RG: John, that sounds similar to Alethea's experience. It was an enlightening experience for you—an experience of love.

JM: I think it happens every time you face your fears and can get through them. That feeling that Alethea had, and that I had, of opposition as you're going through the tunnel, is very common.

RG: That "pressing back" feeling?

JM: The pressing back. She talked about the mist, the heavy mist that she couldn't breathe, the heavy pressure. For me it was the tunnel coming around me. I couldn't breathe. There was a lot of physical pain.

RG: Sounds like confinement.

JM: Very, very, much so, like a birth canal. That's why they liken it to a birth canal.

RG: Going back to the doorway idea for a moment. Now, we talked about doorways and tunnels, so it's like the whole experience for her is the tunnel. The experience of the house, the fear, and finally breaking through—that whole experience that she had is what you're calling "going through the tunnel." In the story—everybody has experienced this in a dream—you're in one place and then suddenly you're in another place. In the story you start up the steps, and at one point she's suddenly up on the landing. This is the way she experienced it. After that she suddenly she gets up to the second floor. And then suddenly she's in the bedroom. And then suddenly she's out there in the field.

It seems that once you experience the "steps," in the transformation, or what I'm calling the "doorways"—when you experience them in a certain way you don't even have to open the door, you just go through.

JM: It is facing and breathing into your fear.

RG: What does "breathing into" mean?

JM: Breathing means you don't stop breathing. You know when you become afraid you hold your breath. You have to keep breathing. And somehow the breathing helps you keep looking at that pressure—the fear that's coming at you. And when you're able to let go of that fear, in other words, not let it bother you anymore, somehow you pop into the next level. This is true. In Zen they call this the Gateless Gate.

51

RG: The *Mumonkan*.

JM: The *Mumonkan*, The Gateless Gate. They are talking about the same thing. The difference is their tunnels are induced by koans, short little sayings that have no meaning that you have to answer. And they build the tension so that the fear builds, and builds, and you have to give an answer. And then all of a sudden you let go of it, and —pop!—you're somewhere else. And you have just passed through the Gateless Gate. It's a very similar process of facing the fear, building the tension, breathing through it and just letting it envelop you. When you can do that it just goes away. You pop out into somewhere else. So Alethea was able to get up to the first landing, and when she could be there, and stay there and relax there, then she was through the gate, and she was on to the next stage.

RG: And there's always a next one.

JM: Always a next one.

RG: Just to recap for a second here. She has to feel the fear, even feel the panic, and somehow maintain her identity and remember who she is, in order to get through the gate, or the doorway.

JM: It's like having a great panic attack. The major method I teach to people with panic attacks is just to breathe through it. You stay with your breath and you just breathe through it. It's like a surfer riding a wave. If you can stay on top of the wave, if you can stay on top of your fear, if you can breathe with your fear, and not fall off the surfboard into the waves and drown, then the wave peaks and ebbs. The fear is the same way. It's just very hard to do that.

RG: In my own experience of panic, when I panic it's like I'm not even there. It's like you're watching yourself panic, and you're frozen. It's a feeling of a loss of identity. It seems to me that part of the process is "sucking it up" and remembering that you are yourself, and you can get through it.

JM: And face it. That's what I call facing your fear.

RG: But there is an identity crisis involved in this.

JM: Yes. I agree. Absolutely. And for some reason Alethea's spirit master, who is trying to contact her in the story, created that fear. I'm not sure why. When Alethea finally let go, and went to the house, she met the lady, and she was fine.

RG: I think you need an obstacle to overcome to prove your greatness.

JM: Or your worth.

RG: As you say, there's some aspect of this also in what now is called building self-esteem. That was not her goal, to build self-esteem, or to meet a spirit master, or anything. She just wanted to get out of it.

JM: She wanted to be able to sleep at night. That's all she wanted to do. She didn't care about anything else. All she wanted to do was to be able to go to sleep, and wake up the next morning and feel good. That's all. That's just where this led her. In the process of the whole thing it changed her, too.

RG: From the point of view of other kinds of problems that people might have, it could be any excess of a feeling that stops you. Alethea had dreams, but some people, for instance, could be just so afraid that they can't leave the house during the day. Another person could be so sad that he can't proceed with his life. It could be a different emotion.

JM: Absolutely. It's usually fear.

RG: It's something you have to face, though.

JM: Something you have to face that feels bigger than you.

RG: In order to live we have to grow. And in order to grow we have to change. So when we're changing there's fear involved of losing who we are. In other words that's a gateway to the next stage.

JM: It's all very archetypal and mythical. And the beauty of this is that you go through it yourself.

RG: One of the amazing parts of the story was the way that you helped her. You were going through this right along with her. And she knew that

53

she had that help.

JM: I can't tell you how I do that. But when the vision on her part is strong enough, I can find it, and I can be there too. It's sort of like having a locus in four-dimensional space. Somehow I can find it. That's what I do. I just waited for her, and then we went there together.

RG: I'm curious about what you just said. You found her place, then you waited for her to appear?

JM: No, I wait for her to go there, then I follow her. Wherever she is, I go there with her. It's like she took me to the house. I didn't know where the house was when she came to me. But as she described the house to me, she took herself back to that place. As she did that I could be there too.

RG: Then you can find that later without her.

JM: Absolutely. And the problem with the whole thing is that what she's experiencing, I experience too. So, it's not some fun little trip that we've got here. All the pain and the terror that she experienced, I also experienced. It's interesting that I can do that, but it's not necessarily the most rewarding thing—until we get to the end!

RG: John, there was another experience that has some similarities to this that you have mentioned to me. This involved a young girl of approximately fourteen that had gone into a severe depression. Her parents had explored every medical and therapeutic option, with no results. And finally they got a referral to come to you. This was during your apprenticeship. Could you relate that story from the point of view of your experience of the tunnel, and the transformation process?

JM: Certainly. Terry was referred to me by the nurse in her daughter's middle school. Terry's daughter, Sarah, at age fourteen suddenly developed severe pain in the front of her left shoulder. Sarah became extremely depressed. They had put her on an anti-depressant, to no avail. They had done every possible medical test on her shoulder, and there was nothing wrong physically with her. However, she was in very severe, sharp pain. As a last resort, Terry brought Sarah to me for acupuncture.

I could tell by looking at Sarah that her shoulder pain was not only physical. She was very depressed, withdrawn, sunken, and pale. I questioned Terry and Sarah, and there was nothing in Sarah's life to explain the situation. Her father had not lost his job. Her parents seemed to be happily married. There were other children in the family that had no problems. There were no deaths. There was no suicide at her school. She had no injury to her shoulder. She was not athletic. She was not playing any sports. She had not fallen. Up to this point Sarah had been a good student. There was no reason for anything like this to happen. There was no emotional or physical trauma, just pain.

This was early in my apprenticeship, so I called my teacher to ask her advice. As usual, she told me a story of what this was all about, and explained what I would have to do to heal Sarah. Whether these stories were true or not was meaningless to me. She drew a picture of something that I had to work through. And when it was done the patient would be healed, and I would have changed. By experience I had come to accept the validity of my teacher's descriptions, and I would just follow the advice she gave.

My teacher said that in a past life Sarah was my granddaughter. At age fourteen she was taken from me and tortured. A hook was stuck in her left shoulder, and she was hung from a tree and left to die. It took her three days to die. I had to find her, climb up into the tree, get her off the hook, and bring her down so she could heal. As her grandfather, I had to save and protect Sarah. By changing the past I would affect the future.

In meditation I connected with her spirit, and I journeyed to the tree. It was very dark. The tree was big, black, dark, and hollow. The only way to get up the tree, was to go up through the trunk, because it was shiny, and there were no branches except at the very top, where Sarah was hanging. The hollow tree became a black, lightless tunnel. I climbed up, hand over hand, against a nameless viscous force that was trying to suck me back down. I had an enormous pressure in my chest the entire time, and roaring in my ears. Going up that tree was the most terrifying experience of my life. I soaked through the clothes I was wearing.

It took me a week or more to climb up the tree in my daily meditation sessions. Each day I would begin stuck in the tree in terror, and I would end stuck in the tree in terror. It affected me twenty-four hours a day. When I finally got up to the top of the tree, I saw that I couldn't just let

Sarah down, as I had expected to do. I thought I could untie the rope from the branch and lower her down to the ground, and then I could get the hook out. But I found out that I had to take her off the hook up there in the tree. So I had to reach out, and lift her off the hook. Once I got her off, I carried her back down through the tree trunk. I brought her back out on the ground, and she was healed.

Shortly after that Terry called me and told me that Sarah had awakened without any pain, and her depression had lifted as well. "I don't know what you did, but Sarah has been improving for a week," she told me. "I don't think we will need to return this week for acupuncture." As far as they knew, it was acupuncture that had healed Sarah. I gave her a total of three acupuncture treatments *(a very short course of treatment, ed.).*

Terry and Sarah knew nothing of the journey I made to the tree. Based on my reading of the situation, and my opinion about the degree of their openness to spiritual subjects, I had decided not to discuss the shamanic journey with them. They came to me for healing, and that is what Sarah received.

RG: In this instance you are going through an initiation, and she is going through a healing. In the shamanic realm you climbed up, and you brought her back down, and somehow bringing her body down healed the flesh-and-blood fourteen year-old girl.

JM: What I saw in that vision was that she had died on that tree at age fourteen, so when she hit that age in this life, the same karmic memory came up in her. So, resolving that karmic situation in the vision somehow transformed her in this lifetime.

RG: In terms of your decision to do the shamanic work without involving the patient directly, that was your practice then, but it would not be your practice now, is that correct?

JM: That's correct. In the beginning of my shamanic healing work I consulted with my teacher on every patient. She would set me out a task— a mythic goal, like finding the Holy Grail.

RG: Your teacher told you that Sarah was in the tree? Or did you find out that she was in the tree?

JM: No, my teacher told me about the past life relationship—that I was Sarah's grandfather, and that she had died in my care. Then I found out about the tree.

RG: So, I'm curious. Now she was fine, and then what happened with you?

JM: I was happy! It worked out fine. It didn't surprise me because once I had brought her down onto the ground I knew she was all better. I sort of wanted to see her one last time to make sure, but I took her mother's word for it. It was transformative for me. Absolutely.

RG: In what ways?

JM: It was another gate to go through. Another fear to overcome. Another something to release. And every time you release these things for people, you change too. They affect you.

RG: Also, it seems to me that you acquired a new skill. Or power.

JM: Yes.

RG: I'd like to talk a little bit about the spirit master that Alethea meets. Here you have someone whose whole life was stopped because of the emotional pain that she was in. And now she goes through this process which also was very painful and arduous, and she meets a spirit master. Who is that?

JM: I was always told that the spirit masters are energetic beings like angels, or like spirits—in my shamanic tradition, ancestors of yours who have died, not necessarily ones from the immediate past. They could be from twenty generations ago, who have come back to help you. So any of that that works for you will work. You could think of it as an angel. You could think of it as an ancestral soul. I found it to be all of it. I've found people have contacted archangels commonly, souls commonly, and spirits.

RG: It's as though the interpretation of what the person is experiencing is colored by their upbringing.

JM: And their cultural background.

RG: Without that cultural stuff, it seems to be a helping influence, or even an extended ability for the person.

JM: It somehow is some energetic presence—whether it's part of you, or separate from you, I'm not sure—that helps you. It gives you a new power. It gives you an intuitive awareness. It opens up a new realm in your existence, in your awareness. And some people like to see them as people, and they talk to them.

RG: There's definitely a communication and connection involved.

JM: Some people feel the connection. Some people hear the connection. Sometimes it's written for people, and they read it.

RG: So it wouldn't necessarily be an individual—like an orange wizard, for example.

JM: No, it's just what you view it as. So, if you read it then it's going to be like a book—this big book that you read. If you hear it, it will be someone talking to you, probably. But sometimes people don't see it as a person talking to them. They might go into a room, or a cave, or a grove—where they hear voices—like God from above, or just voices telling them. Sometimes a tree in a grove will talk to them. And other people don't hear anything—they feel it. They go to a certain place and they feel something that they know is right. So somehow it's an added dimension to them. It gives them a new avenue of exploration, a new energy, a new power, a new way of looking at something.

RG: Going back to the birth idea from before, the person is born into an enlarged definition of his or her identity and abilities.

JM: I would agree with that. And opening up to it is transformative.

RG: Actually, as I reflect upon it, what's happening in most of the stories that we're telling is that the person goes through a very painful period, and the resolution turns out to be much more than just what someone would ordinarily call "healing." There's growth involved.

JM: Correct. It changes your whole being. Somehow you're evolving, for whatever purpose you want to use that for. Abraham Maslow called it a peak experience. In Zen they call it satori, or an awakening experience. But somehow it changes your outlook on things.

RG: Alethea's story is that she "popped out" into a beautiful landscape and met a beautiful spirit guide. Somebody else's experience might be very different. It might not even be visual. But he or she would still experience a transformation. I just want to make it clear that we're not trying to promote "spirit guides."

JM: Nope. That's just what happened.

RG: I'm going to be very specific and explicit about this. If someone were to knock on your door, and say, "I want to meet my spirit guide," it might not happen that way. You never know what's going to happen.

JM: Absolutely. You never know.

RG: This is not something you can pay money to go get. It's an experience in your life that you have.

JM: And some people are ready for it, and some are not. You see a lot of falsehoods in this "out there" today. You know, finding your spirit guides, and your spirit animals, and your spirit this—and all that kind of stuff. Some of it's true, and some of it's not. But it's not something you can just decide, "I want my spirit guide today," and it will happen. That's just not the way it works. Alethea was not looking for it. I was not looking for it when it happened to me. It just happens. I had no control over it. She had no control over it. All she had control over was she faced her fear. And all I knew when I was there with her on the stairs was that we had to keep going up the stairs. We had to keep going through the tunnel, and it would take us somewhere. Where? I had no idea.

RG: Your principle with Alethea was to get her to start moving, and to keep moving.

JM: And to be there with her giving her the strength to do it. I was her guide. I knew the route. I'd been up the stairs before—not those particular stairs, but down tunnels and up stairs, very similar, in the past. I could see what she had to do, and I could be there for her. I could see it with her. I could go there with her. What was going to happen in the end? I had no idea! I knew somewhere she'd come out of the tunnel. What that was going to look like—I had no idea.

Chapter 3

Shamanic Intervention

$\mathcal{D}aniel$

It was December and Dad was severely depressed. When I spoke with him on the phone, he surprised me with an unprecedented resonant baritone voice, in contrast to his usual barely audible conversational style. I knew instantly that he was going through something I had never seen before. He told me that he had woken up at night with a loud cracking noise inside his head. He had been dizzy and had fallen on the way to the bathroom, and the disorienting effects of "the dream," as he called it, had not worn off by morning. He said, "Is this how we grow old, Dan, suddenly, and all at once?" I didn't have any answer. But I did think he was exaggerating. Sadly, I was very wrong about this.

The family doctor sent Dad to a neurologist, who treated his symptoms with medication. He told Dad he would be monitoring his condition, and asked him to return in several weeks to see how the medication was affecting his balance and coordination. There was no specific diagnosis of a particular illness.

I kept in touch with Dad through the winter, speaking with him on the phone several times a week. He continued to be depressed, and he had a low level of energy. Most of the time I could barely hear him speaking, and it seemed like he was having difficulty forming his thoughts—there would be long pauses in the conversation. I was getting quite worried about him.

Sometime in February, to my surprise, he brought up the subject of an upcoming surgical procedure for his enlarged prostate. His condition was not life-threatening, but it was advanced, and the urologist wanted him to have the operation sooner rather than later. I was very concerned about the situation, since I knew he was very depressed, and I felt he would heal better if he postponed the operation until the spring. I discussed this with him, to no avail, and he scheduled the surgery for later that winter, in March. He called the operation "his birthday present," and said he was looking forward to it.

As Dad was making arrangements to have the surgery done, he asked the neurologist if there would be any reason to discontinue the medication he had prescribed during the course of the surgery. He was told that he should continue to take it. However, Dad made the decision on his own to discontinue the medication and he said to me, dramatically, "I flushed the pills down the toilet." There was nothing I could do about this, but I asked him again to consider postponing the surgery until the spring. However, he proceeded with the surgery plans, having been assured by the surgeon that the normal recovery time was about six weeks. That was mid-March. I stayed in touch with him on the phone frequently, at times daily, after his surgery, making several trips to see him that spring.

He seemed to appreciate the attention and concern, up to a point, but as time wore on he began to abruptly change the subject when I would ask about his health. He was clearly getting tired of being a patient, and being a "sick father." His physical recovery from the operation was considerably more protracted than he had expected. The operation itself was, in fact, successful. And local healing directly related to the operation proceeded well. However, the whole experience of his winter depression and the operation took its toll on his overall condition. In late spring he still remained depressed, and he was, at seventy-five, facing what he felt was an enforced retirement. He was not happy, and he was not being treated for his neurological condition.

Nevertheless, I had my own limits as well, and as summer approached, I took my cue (which I would later regret) from Dad, when he complained about getting "too many gifts." I scaled back my calls to him, and went about my business, maybe calling several times a month.

I went to visit my parents around my birthday in mid-to-late August. I took one look at my father, and he was emaciated. He had lost maybe thirty or forty pounds in two months. The last time I had seen him he was overweight. He wasn't fat at that time, but he was a little husky. I wasn't used to him being husky because when I was a kid he was kind of lithe. Now he was just a stick. And I looked at him, and I tried to decide what to do. I finally spoke to him, and said, "Dad, have you been to the doctor?"

He said, "Oh yeah. I was there five weeks ago, and I'm supposed to go back in six weeks."

"What do you mean?" I asked him. I was really alarmed now..

"Well, the doctor checked me out, and he told me to come back in six weeks," he answered, a little peevishly.

I said, "Dad, there's something really wrong here. You've got to go to that doctor, or go to another doctor, right away!"

Dad was simply shrinking away. He was winking out before my eyes. In fact, I was certain that he was dying. I hadn't seen him since June, and it was now August. There he was, standing in the kitchen of his house, literally a shadow of his former self. I couldn't believe how much weight he had lost in such a short time. And he seemed so hesitant, so physically diminished. I could hardly hear him when he spoke. I was absolutely aghast, and I expressed my feelings to him and Mom, but the change had been so gradual for them that they didn't even believe me. I couldn't get them to agree to take any action. I came back from the weekend, and they had just stonewalled me.

Back in Massachusetts I went shopping, and sent Dad a package including better multi-vitamins and a case of canned food supplement. And I kept calling and asking him to see a doctor. Even after a week of calls, he and Mom still wouldn't agree to make an appointment. At that point I spoke to John Myerson, a shamanic healer whom I thought might be able to help. I met with John, explained the situation, and he asked for some specific information about Dad. He said he would do what he could, and he'd let me know in a couple of weeks.

In the meantime I kept up my phone campaign to get Dad to a doctor, preferably a different one than he had already seen. It occurred to me that Dad had another doctor, a specialist whom he had known for years, and really trusted. I thought that if I could get Dad to see this specialist, that doctor would see the danger Dad was in, and would give a referral that Dad would take seriously. I started asking Dad for permission to call the specialist. For a week or more Dad stubbornly resisted my request. However, he agreed to take the food supplement, over Mom's objections. Then one evening I again brought up the subject. Inexplicably, Dad's whole attitude had changed. He agreed that he was in dire need of medical help. He agreed to let me get him an appointment with his specialist friend. And he agreed to see a different doctor on referral from the specialist.

I called John the next morning and gave him the news. "It's an unbelievable, dramatic improvement, from one day to the next," I exclaimed to John. "I've been speaking to him every night. It's like he woke up to the real danger in his situation. Now I can finally hear his voice. And he actually agreed to see another doctor, a decision I've been trying to get him to make for three weeks. He agreed to let me call someone for a referral."

At my next appointment with John I asked him what had been going on from his point of view. John said, "I remember when I called on his soul the first time, I couldn't find him. When I call on a soul usually the scene shifts. What's it like? It's sort of like dialing up an Internet address. All of a sudden the computer screen changes. It isn't gradual. It's all of a sudden. It just goes "BING!" That's what happens to me. It usually changes suddenly, and I'm somewhere else. When I called your father's soul I just got darkness. In fact, I couldn't find him. I thought something was wrong, so I did it again. And I got the same result."

"So, John, that means he was alive, but he was...?" I asked.

"At first I thought he was dead. I thought that he wasn't there anymore. It was very strange to me. But I'm used to strange things because none of this is predictable, you know. Every time you call a soul something has to be done, or interpreted, or felt, or played with. It's never simple. So I had to figure out what the darkness was.

"At first I thought that maybe he just wasn't alive, and I wasn't getting anything. But that didn't make any sense, because if there was a soul I'd find the soul, whether he was alive or he was dead. So, gradually I figured out what the truth was. It actually was darkness. He was just hidden in this darkness. He was in there somewhere, but it was dark—I mean no light, the absence of light completely—just black. This was strange to me, because I usually find something to grab onto. But there was nothing there this time.

"So I decided to see if I could bring some light to the situation. And that's what I did. I just started to put a speck of light somewhere, and I started trying to move the darkness out. And the darkness turned into something that was like heavy ink. It was heavy, weight-heavy. And it wasn't easy to clean up, like ink. You know, when you spill ink, it gets everywhere. That's what this felt like. It was heavy and dark, and it wasn't lifting clearly. But after a while I could get a spot of light, and there was something under it, which I assumed was him!

"Once I had drilled a little hole to see if there was something in there, I had to see if I could pull the cover off. You know, like the old-fashioned camera covers. You would put one hand on top of the drape and pull. Then the whole drape would come off, and there underneath would be the camera. This is what it felt like. I wanted to get the "drape" off, but what I really had to do was to send it away. I had to find a place to send it. It just doesn't disappear, it has to go somewhere, in a specific direction. In this case, it went up and out. So, I found a separate universe and sent the darkness there. It literally pulled off, very slowly, like a cape.

"Then, with the darkness gone, I could see he was condensed, folded in on himself. He was like a fetus, only older. There was no vibrancy. So, I started sending energy and light to him. I surrounded him in light and love, and I just kept sending him light. He wasn't used to light. It was like he had been in a dark cave, and now was suddenly in a bright room. I had to get him to unfold, and from that position stand up and open his eyes. But he was stubborn, and he just stayed there all folded up. I continued to send energy and love, but he didn't move. I tried to embrace him gently. He seemed to be actively ignoring me. So, I had to send him a jolt, and suddenly he woke up. Once he woke up I went back to gently embracing him, and sending light and love, and he started to improve. That was last Tuesday, the day before he agreed to let you help him."

It turned out that Dad had Parkinson's Disease. The specialist gave Dad a referral to his own internist, and he, in turn, sent Dad back to the neurologist, who started the medication again. The extreme weight loss was a symptom of Parkinson's. Over a period of time Dad improved so much that he can now drive locally again, and he has resumed working by his own choice. His condition stabilized. Though Parkinson's is not "curable," recent medical advances have enabled Dad to resume a more normal life. The fact that he changed his mind, and agreed to listen to me and see the specialist, I attribute to John Myerson's intervention.

About two years later I again brought this subject up with John. I asked him, "Did the heavy black substance stay off Dad?"

"It's not there now," John replied.

"What do you think the darkness was?" I asked.

"I didn't feel it was physical, I felt it was entirely mental, or emotional. Probably depression. Depression feels dark and shrunken anyway. And this felt way beyond that, like a whole lifetime was piled up on him, or maybe lifetimes. Because when I got it off he was all shriveled up in the fetal position, and he wouldn't respond," John said.

"All this sounds just exactly like my father to me. There's nothing at all out of whack with your description," I stated.

John answered, "The kind of healing that I do is mainly subtle. So it's going to be psychological, emotional, psychic. The idea being that if you can change something on that level, you can change it on the others."

I said to John, "My opinion is that the changes he underwent as a result of your intervention set him up so that he was able to deal with the Parkinson's."

John answered, "He was shrinking into himself. It's good that you found him at that point. I think he just would have killed himself."

"I think he was dying. When I saw him I thought he was dying. I was really very upset. My parents thought I was nuts," I said.

"Nothing unusual. They always think you're nuts, anyway, right?" John laughed.

"The thing that is amazing to me, John," I said, "is that in the next few months after your intervention, Dad said things to me that I never, ever, would have expected. He communicated directly with me in a positive, direct person-to-person way. At one point he actually thanked me for saving his life."

A Conversation with John Myerson on Shamanic Intervention

This interview was conducted by Robert Greenebaum with shamanic healer John Myerson.

RG: John, to many people the Daniel's story would seem quite incredible. Here, this man comes to you, and he says, "I think my father's dying and it's just because he won't take care of himself. Is there anything you can do?" And, without having met the father you then locate him in what you call four-dimensional space, and you go help him. Now, you've also described this as a traditional shamanic healing, because the patient is not doing it with you. What is the attitude that you take in a traditional shamanic healing? And what is involved for you? How do you manage to accomplish these things?

JM: Well, traditionally—and by "traditionally" I mean in the past, and in cultures where shamanic traditions are still very strong—healing involves a procedure, or process, that a shaman would use to journey to another realm, see what a problem is, either get information or fix it, and then come back again. So, traditionally the patient would be, for instance, lying there next to the shaman, or sitting there with the shaman, or not even with the shaman—and the shaman would drum, would take psychotropic drugs, would dance, would sing—would do something that gets him or her into that altered state—the shamanic healing state. And then, in that state, the shaman would have visions, or go places, or whatever it is that they see or do that helps people heal. That's what I did with Daniel's father, but without the drum, or drugs, or any prescribed external activity.

Sometimes people come to me and possibly someone is dying, or whatever the case may be, and there's nothing I can do. You know, the person is old, they're dying, they have cancer, or whatever the story may be. It's a physical thing. It's time for them to go, and there's nothing I can do. Other times I go there, and I can see that the soul is already separated. And, there again, there's nothing I can do. And other times I'm lucky enough to be able to see, or feel, or experience something, and I'm able to help in the situation.

And traditionally, I would say, shamans talk about it as almost like a battle—between good and evil, light and dark—opposing forces. And as someone who does this work, I have to be able to use both of those abilities—I have to be able to work with love and light and healing energy—on the other hand I also have to have strength and power to be able to work with, or defeat, or move away, or heal, or whatever the other energy is that I need to come up against. In general, in cases like this, it's not pleasant. For example, the energy that was around Daniel's father was not to his benefit at all. It was killing him. For whatever reason, it was there, and it was not something that you go up and touch and say, "Hi. How're you doing? You want to move away please?" (laughs) It just doesn't work that way. So you can call it "evil," if you like. Or you can call it "dark." Or you can call it whatever you want to call it. (laughs again) And in some cases they will turn around and attack you, the person trying to heal. So you have to be ready for all kinds of things. So, really it's like a mini kind of battle.

RG: Mini? It doesn't sound very "mini" to me!

JM: "Mini" meaning that it's me and "it." It's not like huge throngs and warfare. (laughs)

RG: Did you have to use a "physical" force with Daniel's father?

70

JM: Yes. As the story tells, the first part of the problem was that I couldn't find him. The whole thing was dark. I liken it to dialing up a Web site, and you get a blank screen. It felt like that, except it was pitch black. It was just black, there was no light. And I did it a couple of times so I knew he was there somewhere, because if he had died I still would have been able to contact his soul. So something would have still been there. So, I knew this wasn't good to begin with. Any time you get into a dark place like that it's not good. Just to make that little bit of light, that little bit of light I talked about—to see if he was even there—I needed to use power to do that. And when I speak of power, I'm not talking about power "over" somebody. I'm not talking about an evil kind of thing. I'm talking about an energy that I have to use, when I have to use it, to exert force on something that's not going to move.

RG: As an example, you could have nuclear weapons, or you could have radiation therapy. It's still radiation. The power is neutral, and you use it based upon your attitude...

JM: ...yes, my attitude. And each shaman will have his or her own gift, his or her own power, his or her own way of doing it. Mine takes the form of a sword, and I wield it in those other realms. So that's what I did here. I used it to make a "hole," and to see what was there.

RG: When you are wielding this power sword—as you're describing it—it's not as if you're cutting things up. I'm really curious as to what your attitude is in relation to your actions.

JM: Given the choice, I will always use love and light first. The guiding principle in my life is always what I refer to. It comes out of Buddhism— the Mahayana Boddhisatva ideal, which is to help, heal, and serve others—to make an offering of myself. And I would like to use that energy as much as I can. Sometimes, however, what you come up against is too strong and too dark for that. But if you can stay centered in that place of light and love, the energy that you use, and the energy that you wield, will come from that place, and it doesn't harm either myself, or whatever I'm doing it to. The tendency in this, and the problem with doing shamanic work like this, is that you can get addicted to the power. Because, obviously the more power that you build up, the stronger you're going to be. But, for me, if I don't have that base of the Boddhisatva ideal, and the offering of myself, and the love, then I get addicted to that power—that energy, that strength. And then I become unbalanced. So, I use it reluctantly, because I don't want to get addicted to that.

RG: To clarify for people who are not familiar with it, my understanding of the Boddhisatva ideal is that an individual who spiritually transcends this physical reality will then make a conscious decision to stay in this physical reality and help other beings. Is that how you understand it?

JM: Yes—through light, love, and compassion. And I'm not saying that I'm a Boddhisatva. I'm not saying I died and was reborn on purpose. All I'm saying is that from my Buddhist training that is the part that I identify with the most. And I've used it as a cornerstone in my life—to make that offering, as a Boddhisatva would—to help others.

RG: Now this is what you also call "connecting to the universe with love." Could you explain that principle?

JM: The energy of love is the guiding principle in the universe. It is what most religions are based on, and it is what I base all my healing on. And what I mean by that is to let the love that's in the universe flow through me, so that I feel a spiritual connection to everything around me. But, it's also a physical connection. It happens on the body-mind-spirit spectrum. And I try to base all my healing on that place of love, and try to come from that place of love all the time.

RG: Actually, what you say is, "connecting to the universe with love." What occurs to me is that you're making a choice and deciding what your relationship with the universe is going to be. And when I say "you," I mean anybody. To me that is the healing part. Based on what I've heard from you, my own conclusion is that you can't really separate it into parts—it's only words that are "love" or "healing." They're not exactly the same, but are almost identical. Would you agree with that?

JM: Yes.

RG: It's a choice and a relationship foundation.

JM: And people have a choice in their lives, of how they want to run their lives. They can run their lives based on fear, or they can run their lives based on love. And what I try to do is base my life on love. And to the extent that I can get others to feel that love, healing will happen instantaneously. And you notice, in a lot of the stories that we're telling, when a person comes to that place of light and love, healing happens. In the case of Daniel's father I had to bring him to that place. The situation was too serious. If he had been here, and I had talked to him about love, he wouldn't have heard it. So, for me it was a life and death situation, literally. He was dying. I took matters into my own hands, and tried to get him to feel the love. And when he could feel the light and the love, he changed.

RG: It also occurs to me that when you were talking a few minutes ago about using a sword—that can be a pretty scary image, depending upon how you look at it. But if you think of it as a "warrior of light," sort of like Ivanhoe, wielding "The Sword of Power for Love and Goodness", that's the kind of image you're presenting to me.

JM: And again, it's a very archetypal symbol. All through Western mythology in our culture there are knights in shining white armor wielding the sword of power of God and love.

RG: Does that feel like an appropriate image in relation to what you're doing? Or is there something different or additional there?

JM: I don't see myself that way. I just see myself as being very practical. And I use what I have to use, when I have to use it, to help somebody get to that place of love and light. And if I need to use force to do that, then I do it. But my choice is always the other.

RG: The whole concept of being pragmatic, though, is again one of those neutral concepts. You can be pragmatic and "take people out," or you can be pragmatic and help people heal. So...

JM: Good point! (laughs) That's a very good point. That's true. I try not to take anybody out. That's not my thing. (laughs again) And traditionally shamans did do things like that. They worked for their people, and their villages, and their tribes—everything can be used both ways.

RG: Let's talk about a few more examples of times when you have made the decision to take the traditional shamanic route, as opposed to working with the person—possibly because the person wasn't there. Or you were being asked by a third party. Let's talk about any of those situations.

Actually, one of the situations I remember concerns a woman whose boyfriend broke up with her as she left for an extended trip abroad. She went away for over a year, and she thought she was leaving home with a boyfriend who was in love with her, and they were going to stay in touch with each other. He never showed up at the airport, and later e-mailed her that he was moving on, and had a new girlfriend. She was devastated. She was e-mailing back and forth with a friend who knew you, and the friend suggested that she ask you to do a separation between her and the boyfriend so she could get on with her work, and her life in the new place. The boyfriend was local, but in a location unknown to you, and she was abroad.

JM: Yes, for this one I didn't know the boyfriend, and I didn't know the woman. I just heard of the woman through her friend. There was nothing evil or life-threatening happening to the woman who was in Europe requesting the separation. However, it was affecting her emotional health, and it was affecting her ability to do her job that was the purpose of her trip. If she had been here with me I could have psychologically done some therapy, and we could have come to some place that was different, but in this case I had no face-to-face contact with her. So, I just moved the two of them away from each other. And in this situation, I just had the two of them—in the shamanic realms—connect to the universe with love and let go of each other. It was very peaceful. It was very beautiful. It involved love. It involved me being forceful enough to talk to the two of them so they would let go of each other, but there was no other power involved, just the love.

RG: Did you actually have a dialog with them?

JM: Well, mainly with the boyfriend. And then she couldn't let him go. She wanted to let him go, but couldn't let him go.

RG: If you were to say in conversation what you said to them, what would it have been? In other words, could you summarize what you said to her, and what you said to him?

JM: Remember this wasn't in words... To him I would say, "Look, you hurt her. Your actions with her were very hurtful." And I would say to her that, "I know he hurt you, but the only way for you to really get over this is to let him go—is to forgive him, have him admit that he hurt you—and you forgive him, so that you can move on, and he can move on, and the two of you can live the rest of your lives." So the first step was getting him to say, "I'm sorry I hurt you." And her to say, "OK, I do forgive you." And then just getting them to separate. Because, you see, there was no darkness in this. He was not trying to be evil. He was not trying to control her, hurt her on purpose, manipulate her, or use power over her, or any of that kind of stuff. He made a mistake.

RG: I think there was another story that you mentioned to me, of a woman who actually was involved in an incestuous relationship with her grandfather?

JM: Yes.

RG: That does sound very dark to me.

JM: Here's the story. Noelle first came to me with lower abdominal pain. She did not have colitis or irritable bowel disorder. Just a sharp pain. She was suffering from this for a few years. Noelle had ultrasound and an MRI but nothing showed up on the tests. She came to me on a recommendation of her sister's friend who had been a patient of mine.

We began with acupuncture, since that is what she came for. I told her that I thought there was something else going on with her that might be causing the pain. She appeared to have a blackness to her that was very obvious to me. However, I needed to gain her trust, so we began treatments.

Noelle got some improvement over the course of a month but after she went home to visit her family for Christmas it got much worse. I thought this would be a good time to sit down and talk.

She had meditated in the past and was familiar with my work from her sister's friend. This made it easier for me to work with her. I told her about the blackness that I saw. I felt that it had a masculine feeling and that this feeling usually came from some kind of trauma or abuse in the past. I felt whatever and whomever caused this blackness was the cause of her pain. It needed to be released so she could heal.

The first session of this type was not too intense, more like descriptive. Noelle told me about her grandfather. She grew up in a city in

Ohio. In the summers she and her sister used to spend a lot of time with her mother's parents on their farm in Wisconsin. Her grandfather sexually molested her from about age 8 to 14 when she was strong enough to end it. I had her do a separation with him as a beginning of the healing.

The next session was intense. Her grandfather was here in the room with us. His presence was very strong and we both could sense and see him. He was dark, stern, domineering, and very angry at both of us. He was angry at Noelle for trying to break away and with me for bringing this up. He had passed away a few years back but in the shamanic realms he was still attached to Noelle and wanted to stay that way. He wanted this because he got energy from the connection with her and wanted to stay connected so when Noelle died he could still possess her.

I had Noelle work on the separation when we were apart in the usual way. However, I would work on this also. When I entered the shamanic realms and called on the soul of her grandfather, he would come and try to scare me. It felt like a dark, evil, strong being of energy attacking me, trying to push me away. Like a black bird chasing a hawk away from its territory. My nature is to try to get behind the attack so I can see what he is protecting. I felt the strangest thing. It felt to me as though he was part of a chain stretching back many generations. Like he was trying to initiate Noelle into some black family cult through his sexual abuse. I could see all the beings in this cult back many generations lined up behind her grandfather.

When I told her this she was shocked but not surprised. She said the abuse always had a ritualistic quality to it and that he was always telling her that he was doing this so she could join "them." I asked her to question her mother about this. She had told her mother about the abuse a few years ago but her mother was sort of ambivalent and asked her: "Are you sure, dear?" I urged her to question her mother further.

The next week Noelle told me that her mother confessed that she had also been abused by her grandfather when she was a little girl. I decided then and there that it was time to end this string of sexual abuse in the family by cutting the ties that bound Noelle and her grandfather and sending him to the light so that he would not bother her again in this lifetime or any other.

The next day, as I entered the shamanic realms, I called all of my spirit guides and masters to me to help give me strength. In these types of encounters, one needs as much power as one can have. Otherwise the battle-like scene will not work in my favor. It is all about power and love. You need the power for strength and you need the love and light to battle the darkness. When I called on his soul, he expected me to meet him head on to try to overpower him. Instead, I surrounded him in light and kept the intensity of the light high. I kept this up until I was able to shrink his energy field and then I began to move him away. I kept at it until he was gone. The next day when I called on his soul, he did not come.

The next week Noelle looked different. She was radiant and her blue eyes shown with a light that was not there before. By the end of the month, she was pain-free.

RG: To some people, John, this would seem like you were police, judge, and jury. How could someone be certain that you were going to be doing this appropriately?

JM: Well, I think that's the problem with shamanic activity in general. You can't know. You have to rely on the person you're working with. I try to act in a way that does nobody harm, that does no harm at all. And I try to act in a way that's—as I've said before—loving, and uses only love, and is for the healing benefit of the person who has requested my help. To start with, obviously the grandfather didn't benefit, but on the other hand Noelle came to me needing help, and if I hadn't done that, then she wouldn't have been able to heal. So I did use my judgement in sending him away, which maybe was not the best for him, but to me that was evil that he was doing.

RG: So, maybe a more appropriate way of looking at it would be that you become a powerful advocate for the person who's requesting the healing services.

JM: Yes, and one of the things that happens to me is whenever I meet people I can tell there are things going on with them. Normally, I don't investigate, I don't look, I don't heal. I haven't been asked. So I don't do anything. Everything I've discussed here, I've been asked to do. Daniel came to me and asked me for help for his father. Noelle came to me and asked me for help. And so I help.

RG: And in the case of the woman who was on the trip, she asked for help. That seems to be a necessary component of the relationship of a patient to the healer. There has to be a request.

JM: I'm not sure there has to be a request. But, energetically, you're going to burn out real fast if you just do it all the time. So, I limit myself to people who ask me for help—and also to help that I can give.

RG: It sounds like it's part of your "code."

JM: Part of my code. Yes. And also, sometimes when people ask, they are not ready. So, either they have to get to a place of being ready to be helped, or you have to wait.

RG: Another aspect of this is the fact that the people that you are helping may not be physically with you at the time, or that the other person is definitely not there physically. Especially in the story about Daniel, his father was not with you. He was several hundred miles away. How are you able to do that?

JM: What I do is, I liken it to a Web address, in four dimensions. You have to have the—shall we say—coordinates to find the person. And I use information of the person's name, I use their birthday, I use a picture of them—it could be any of these. And I use the mind of the person who's here with me. So, in the case of Daniel, he had a picture in his mind of his father. And through that I could connect to his father—through Daniel's mind. I never met Daniel's father. I never saw a picture of Daniel's father, so I actually don't physically know what he looked like. But, through Daniel I could connect to him. That's how I did it in that case. And that's what I do. I call it "Calling the Souls." It's something that I do in my head. I call the soul, and I get a "ping" or a feeling.

RG: Once you have the location of the soul, you can contact that soul whenever you want to?

JM: It's like having the phone number.

RG: Again, in the story of Daniel, it sounds like he didn't want to answer the phone.

JM: Yeah. That was a unique one, of calling, and finding nothing but darkness. That was unusual. That was an interesting one. And that threw me. I thought that I had done something wrong. You know none of these are the same. Every time you call a soul you get something different. So, you have to be sort of alert as to what you're throwing yourself into. (laughs)

RG: Is it like coming into the other soul's reality—into their vicinity?

JM: I'm not sure if I travel at all. I don't feel I travel at all. I just feel I have a connection to them. It's like e-mail with a visual—video mail, or something. It feels to me like it's a tube. And I get a feeling or a picture of what's happening.

RG: I wonder if that ability to go through the tunnel is directly related to the ability to make this kind of contact.

JM: I would think it's exactly the same thing. And being able to contact the person repeatedly is just like going through the tunnel. Once you've been through a tunnel, and you get to a certain place on the other side, you can always go back to that place via the tunnel. And the same is true of calling the souls. Once I've contacted the person, I can always go back there the same way. It's like getting a road map.

RG: In the case, for instance, of Noelle's grandfather—where he's definitely an unsavory character—does he try to spread that junk on you through the connection?

JM: Well, as I said in the story, Noelle's grandfather tried to attack me. And, in the beginning he felt me, and he ignored me—kind of like I was a mosquito buzzing around. And then when he realized that there was something here, he paid attention to me. And then one time he literally came at me. And that's when I used the sword. I brought the sword out and stopped him. And then, instead of using the sword, what I tried to do with him was just shrink him with the love. Because he was so dark, and so massive, I just felt I would blanket him with light. And what he did was shrink inside the light. He didn't like the light. He didn't like the feeling of it. So he made himself smaller,—and smaller, and smaller. And when he got real small, I just was able to handle him. I didn't think of this, you know. This is not planned. This just happens. These are instantaneous happenings. When he came at me it was not slow, and it wasn't planned, and I didn't see it coming. However, I was certainly ready for it.

RG: In that regard, it's just like a real battle.

JM: It's just like a real battle.

RG: Can you be harmed if they...

JM: Absolutely, no question. And I've been made sick. And I've been hurt from getting in over my head. Then I have to retreat—and heal.

RG: And go back and finish the job.

JM: Right, or call in reinforcements! (laughs)

RG: Is that when you call in the spirit masters?

JM: Well, I always do that anyway. And without any question—that's where I get my energy and power from. And I'll definitely have to call in more spirit masters. Or I'll have to go back and eat my Wheaties and my spinach! In this business you can't do too much of this because you get literally burnt out very quickly.

RG: As you gain experience, can you gauge how much effort you're going to have to expend on a given case? Or can you never tell that?

JM: I very rarely can tell. I knew Noelle's grandfather was dangerous, but I didn't think he would turn on me. I didn't think he would come at me like that. That part was a surprise for sure. And I've had other ones like that. I can remember one person—I was cleaning her aura. In other words, in her aura there was a crack. And I was trying to help seal that, because her energy was leaking out that way. And I didn't perceive it when I was doing this—I was using light and love, and healing the aura—and I guess it was a dark thing that was attached to that crack in the aura. Maybe it was feeding, maybe it was getting the energy out of it. Anyway, whatever it was, I didn't see it. And it came right at me. So, it's sort of like walking into a barn, and all of a sudden the bats come at you. Really sudden, and really dark. And it startles you. So you have to get your protection up real fast! (laughs) But I just sort of deflected it, and it went away. But if I hadn't been strong enough to deflect it, it would have attached to me.

But I think, for me, the idea of connecting to the universe with love is the central thing that I try to do. Through all the darkness, and all the evil grandfathers, and all that kind of stuff, if I can help somebody get to that place—that place of being able to feel the light and the love, and the energy of the universe passing through them—then I've succeeded, and they're on their way to wherever they're going—living a better, fuller life.

Chapter 4

Healing from Spiritual Interference

Tracy

I just couldn't get pregnant no matter what I did. The doctors, including my gynecologist and two fertility specialists, had no answer except, "Keep trying, Tracy, don't give up." According to all the exams, and the tests they had run I was A-OK. On the other hand, my best friend, Liz, said I was trying too hard. I don't think she even knew how right she was. But I sure found out later. What there was no question about, at all, was that I was going nuts with worry. And I was really frightened that I wasn't going to get pregnant at all, and Lewis and I never would have a child of our own.

Lewis and I were married nearly five years ago, in Chicago, and we moved to Boston the following year, for his new job. I found a new job in Massachusetts, too. We waited to have kids because we thought we should get to know each other really well before becoming parents, and we wanted to save some money first. So it wasn't until a year and a half ago that we started trying. It was fun at first, with the anticipation every month. But when I didn't get pregnant after the first four or five months, I got scared and went to the doctor—without telling Lewis, of course. He wasn't too troubled by the situation, being a sort of happy-go-lucky guy, but I was really spooked. Dr. Knowles checked me out, and the answer he gave me was, "No problems. Just keep on doing what you're doing, and don't worry. Sometimes these things take time."

For a while I would just cry my heart out. But after more than a year of "Keep trying," and taking my temperature every day, and all that stuff you have to do, and doctors all the time, and thinking about adoption, then I started getting really hard and steely inside. When my boss offered more work, I took it, just so I wouldn't have to feel so bad all the time, and so I could stay busy, and get something done right. I took a whole string of out-of-town assignments too, and I was gone for a week at a time, and back home for weekends. Altogether, I was spending less and less time with Lewis. When we did spend time together, we'd argue. And the sex was terrible, so biological. I felt like we were breeding. In fact, our marriage was straining to the breaking point. I really needed to figure out what to do. But I didn't really have any ideas.

Another six months went by, with still nothing. During that time I went to two fertility specialists, who tested right and left, up and down, and they both said the same, "No problems. Keep on trying." When he realized how upset I was getting, Lewis got himself checked out, and he was fine too. To my annoyance, he was actually pretty self-satisfied about the test. That put even more pressure on me. I couldn't have been more frustrated, or frightened, or so I thought. I kept wondering what to do. I am not a real religious person, but I started praying for help around then, "God, why are you doing this to me? If you'll just let me have my baby, I'll do anything."

A few more months went by, and now the doctors were talking about artificial insemination, and in vitro fertilization. Even Liz was talking about adoption. I'm really good at research, so I looked into every medical option, but I just felt like a rat in a maze with no way out. Lewis wasn't interested in adopting, and, the truth be told, neither was I. It all seemed so hopeless. I almost felt like just giving up then and there, but something inside told me to hang on.

Even though I swore her to silence, Liz, who is a nurse, told another of her friends about me, and my story made the rounds at her hospital. Eventually someone gave Liz the name of an acupuncturist, and told her that it had worked for someone she knew. I was so desperate for a solution that I called him right away. I left my name and phone number on John Myerson's answering machine that afternoon. He called me back the following day and we spoke briefly. When I asked him if he could help me, he said he had been able to help several women in similar circumstances. Actually, just talking to him felt pretty good, so I said to myself, "What do I have to lose?" And I answered myself, *Nada*. I made an appointment to see him the following week. He seemed very upbeat about the situation, and I found myself looking forward to the appointment, though with a heavy dose of skepticism since nothing had worked so far. In fact, I didn't really know anything about acupuncture at all.

John greeted me with a big laugh, saying, "Come in, Tracy, make yourself comfortable." I couldn't help myself from smiling and feeling some of the tension drain away as I entered his office. When I had sat myself down, without any preliminaries, he just asked me, "OK, Tracy, tell me the problem. What's up?"

"As I mentioned on the phone, John, I can't get pregnant, and there's no medical reason," I said. "I just want acupuncture so I can have a baby. You said it might work. Will it work? Is there a chance?"

"Of course there's a chance, Tracy. I'll do everything I can to help you," John said. "Let's see if we can get you a little more relaxed today. We'll talk a little bit, then you'll have some acupuncture, and I'll prescribe some herbs to help build up your strength. You seem very nervous, but there's really nothing to worry about. I think you'll start feeling better pretty quickly."

John began explaining his course of treatment to me. "Tracy, what I would like to do is to give you several acupuncture treatments over the next few weeks to relax you and build and strengthen your reproductive energy. I also would like you to take some herbs I will prescribe, for the same reason. Would that be OK?"

"Sure, John," I answered. "After all, that's what I came here for."

"Also, Tracy, I have a couple of suggestions to reduce your level of stress. You really have gotten yourself all wound up about this, and I would like you to relax as much as possible about getting pregnant. First of all, stop taking your temperature every day, and have sex because you and Lewis want to, and not just to have a baby, OK? I want you to forget about that part as much as you can."

I felt pretty sheepish and even a bit ashamed, and just said "OK, John, I'll try it your way."

After we talked for awhile more, John took me into his acupuncture treatment room. He had me take off my shoes and lie down on the treatment table. I guess I thought he was going to put needles in my stomach, but he only put a needle in my left ear, and one in each hand and foot. They really didn't feel like anything. To tell you the truth, I just liked being taken care of. He put on some soft music and left the room, saying, "I'll be back in a little while, just let yourself drift off to sleep." I woke up just as he was coming back into the room. It turned out to be a half hour later. I felt really refreshed. He took the needles out, and went back into his office while I put my shoes on. I felt good, so I made another appointment for the following week. He also gave me some powder I was supposed to dissolve under my tongue three times a day. As I left I said to myself, "OK, Tracy, at least you're doing something positive," although I was confused about how the acupuncture and herbs would help.

The next time I went to see John he again made a joke as I came up the stairs. I found myself really liking him. He seemed very confident and sure. After I settled down he began asking a few questions. I told him my story again, a little more detailed. After I finished, he said, "Tracy, you really need to learn how to relax a little with this situation. I know it's frustrating for you. You've been letting the whole situation get out of hand."

I got upset right away. I leaned forward, and almost screamed at him, "But John, I just want to get pregnant!"

"Look at you, Tracy!" he exclaimed. "You're right off the wall. You're not going to get pregnant like this. You're not appealing like this. It's hard to have sex like this. It's hard to enjoy sex like this. Do you really want to bring a child into the world under these conditions? You've lost control of your life, Tracy, and you need to reestablish a sense of reality for yourself!"

At that point I just began sobbing uncontrollably. I felt so frustrated and ashamed of myself. It went on for a long time. How could he say that to me, that I wasn't attractive? On the other hand, he was probably right, and he had said he would help, so I guessed he knew what he was doing. He offered me tissues, and he waited, and slowly I came out of it.

"Tracy," he said, "I want to treat you again today, and then I'll show you a few Yoga stretches you can use to unwind in the morning and evening. Do them with your husband, if he's interested."

I went to see John every week for about a month and a half. Each time he would talk with me for a while, then treat me with acupuncture, and give me a new exercise for that week. I found myself trusting him, and I'm not really that trusting a person. My friends at work were starting to make comments about how I was chilling out and easier to work with. And Liz said she thought I was starting to look good again. Even Lewis noticed a change, and we started going out to dinner again, and movies. I was starting to feel, "Maybe I do have a future."

Then the dreams started. I don't often remember my dreams, but these were different. They were usually about when I was really little, and my mother was pregnant with Linda, my baby sister. I was so looking forward to when she would be born. I was four, and my mother used to let me fall asleep with my head on her lap, and I would imagine I could talk to the baby inside her through her belly. Of course, the baby wasn't Linda yet, so I just used to call her Baby. "Baby, I'm your big sister Tracy," I would say. Or, "When are you coming out, Baby? I want to play with you."

Or I would dream about later, after Linda was born. I would watch her sleeping in her crib. Or when Mom was changing her diaper. She was so cute and tiny—I just couldn't believe how small her fingers and toes were.

Another time I dreamt about my dolls, and how I would pretend that they were my very own babies. I'd change their clothes, and feed them, and sing them to sleep. I always knew I'd get married and have babies. How could I be wrong about that? I hadn't thought about these events in years, probably since they happened. But the dreams were actually pleasant, and when I mentioned them to John, he said he felt it was a good sign. He said, "Things are moving, I like that, Tracy." I didn't really understand, but I thought, "If he's happy, I'm happy, he seems to know what he's doing."

It was maybe the sixth or seventh time I went to see John. I was getting my acupuncture and herbs each week, and I was doing the Yoga stretches he had shown me. Usually we would talk first, and then he would give me my acupuncture treatment. This time I got a real jolt. Once I had got settled he bluntly said, "Tracy, I have to ask you a question. Have you ever had an abortion?"

I was really shocked. I hadn't mentioned it to John, since the doctors at the time said there was nothing from it that would affect my fertility. I got really uncomfortable right away, and started feeling guilty. I could feel my face getting flushed, and my throat starting to choke up.

I blurted out, "Yes, I had an abortion when I was seventeen. My boyfriend, Walt, got me pregnant. My parents wouldn't let me have the baby. I was scared to have the abortion, but they were right, I wasn't ready to be a mother. I wasn't the only girl in my class to have one, either!" And then the tears started, and I just cried my heart out for a long time. When I stopped, John began talking to me.

He said, "That's good news, Tracy. Now we've got something to work on." I couldn't believe my ears. "What in God's name is he talking about?" I thought to myself.

"Listen, Tracy," he continued, "I believe that you have unfinished business in your heart, and in your womb, that needs to be completed before you can have a child. The unfinished business is that the soul of the aborted baby is still with you in some way, and that is blocking your natural ability to get pregnant. Your problem is not medical, as you already know from your doctors."

I was stunned. I thought about it for a few minutes. I asked myself if this really could be the problem. Those events had happened such a long time ago, and I hadn't thought much about it since I got over the sense of loss I had at the time. Not that I really wanted the baby, but I felt sad anyway. It was something in my body. Kind of a wrenching sense of something falling down somewhere inside. But I thought I had got over it. Now my feelings were telling me that John was right. It wasn't over yet. I was almost speechless, but I managed to blurt out, "OK, John, I feel something is right about what you are saying, now that you mention it."

John began explaining to me, "Tracy, at least psychologically, you have to release the soul that was aborted. I am sure you are wondering how you can possibly do that. There is an actual procedure and a process for doing this, and I will help you all the way through it. I believe that once you have gone through this healing process you will be able to have a child."

"I'm feeling pretty rocky from the whole subject," I told John. The tears were right behind my eyes, just waiting to come out again, and my chest felt tight and crampy.

"Listen, Tracy," John said, "we're going to take this one step at a time. I think you are going to feel terrific when we get all the way through. So, let's start now. I want you to go home and spend few minutes a day thinking about your aborted baby. Just think about how you felt at the time. After a while I'd like you to decide whether your baby was a boy or a girl. Come back next week and we will talk about it. In the meantime I want you to remember that I am also working with you every day, and you can call me for any reason at all that you need to talk with me. You are not alone in this. Remember what I'm saying, Tracy. Do you think you can do that?"

I just mumbled, "OK." I certainly didn't feel too sure of myself. And I guess I was sort of frightened about confronting my feelings, and what John called the "soul" of the aborted baby. Could it be real? I asked John, "Is the soul of the baby real?"

"Tracy," John answered thoughtfully, "as far as I am concerned, the soul of the aborted baby is as real as you or me. But, what is important right now is that you are willing to go ahead with the first steps, as I discussed them with you. I think that you will be able to make your own mind up about the soul later. I think you should know that the aborted soul wants to move on as much as you do."

I was really anxious about the whole thing, but everything John had done was really helping me feel a lot better. I had come this far, and I trusted him, so I said, "OK, John, I will go ahead with the steps you are asking me to do, but I have another question. What I want to know is what do you mean that you are working with me every day? I only come here once a week. You mentioned this before, but I never asked you about it."

"Suffice it to say, Tracy, that I am thinking about you every day, and that I am helping you in this way every day. I want you to know that I am actually going through this with you, and I will be helping you go through the process step by step. It may sound mysterious to you, but I am helping you in the name of love. I think you can tell that that is true. If you have any further doubts, I should tell you that later you will be asking the aborted soul for forgiveness. I am certain that you will receive it. Your fears are natural, but you should not let them stand in your way. Do you think you can go ahead with this process?"

I agreed, somewhat reluctantly, and after receiving my acupuncture treatment, which calmed me considerably, I left the office. As I left I noticed that John was very upbeat. He said that he was looking forward to seeing me the next week, and to call if I needed to talk.

That evening at home I began to think about the events surrounding my teenage pregnancy. I hadn't thought about these events for years. In fact, I had believed that I had forgotten the whole miserable experience. But it wasn't so. I could remember everything—how much I had wanted to make love with Walt; how scared I was when we didn't use any protection; the sinking feeling I had when I found out I was pregnant; the pride that I could actually have a baby; how Walt turned his back on me; my parents' shock, and their heavy-handed concern. And I remembered the abortion and the feeling of relief when it was all done with. It all came back to me in a rush. I couldn't get to sleep, and stayed up late watching talk shows until I dozed off towards dawn.

After a few days of remembering these primarily unpleasant events, and re-experiencing those old feelings, I suddenly remembered what John had said. He wanted me to feel whether the baby was a boy or a girl. Once I thought of this I immediately knew that it was a girl.

"Here comes trouble!" John greeted me the next time I went to see him. And then he laughed that big booming laugh he has. I was scared going in, but that broke the ice right away.

"So, Tracy, which is it, boy or girl?" John asked.

I told him that I was sure it was a girl. Then he said, "The next step is to name your baby, Tracy. Did you have a name in mind for the girl baby?"

"No, not really, John," I replied. I actually was a little numb about the whole thing right then.

"Well, that is what I would like you to do this week, name your baby."

We talked about my experiences with Walt and my parents for the rest of the session, and I left wondering what to call my baby girl that I never had.

The following week as I took time to think about the aborted baby each day, more and more details of that time filtered back. At some point I think I just started accepting the reality of it. I never really did that before. I guess I just buried the whole subject. It had never occurred to me that I was preserving all those feelings by doing that.

I started thinking of names, and it was really difficult. Finally, I decided on May, because that's when most of the events happened. Once I had the name, it was easier to feel that she was real. Suddenly I knew what John had meant when he said the soul was real. At first I was all excited, and then the tears came again. For hours and hours all I could do was cry. I even took the next day off from work, since I felt too upset to be with anyone.

When I told John about it at our next session he was ecstatic, grinning and grinning until I couldn't stand it any more. "John, why are you so happy about this?" I exclaimed.

"Well, Tracy," he replied, still grinning, "I'm so happy for you. You have come a long way very quickly."

"What do you mean, John?" I asked, feeling pretty dumb, actually.

"In only a couple of weeks you have opened up a very old wound, and you are well on your way to healing it. That's why you're here, isn't it? So, I'm happy! If you don't feel it yet, don't worry, you will soon enough."

"That's great, John." I said, without much conviction. "Is that it? Are we done with the healing process you described?"

"No, Tracy, we're not done yet, but we've come a long way. And you have done really well. How do you feel?" John asked, opening his arms.

"I guess I feel pretty good," I answered. "She wasn't real to me before, not really, just sort of a vague bad thing in my life that I wanted to forget about. Now I think that I can look back and see the mistakes I made, and I certainly can remember those events a lot better."

"That's right, Tracy. You have reclaimed a very big part of yourself. If you think about it, I bet you even feel more energetic than you have recently. That's the freed-up energy that was tied up in these memories and bad feelings. That's why I feel so happy about it. Now we can move on to the next step," John said.

"What's the next step, John?" I asked, feeling a little anxious again.

"This week," John replied, "I'm going to give you a separation prayer that I want you to say every day."

John dictated the prayer to me, and I wrote it down. The prayer said I was to call on May's soul and ask her to release me. I was to send her love and I was to forgive her.

"I want you to continue to spend a few minutes each day thinking about May, and either read the prayer silently, or speak it aloud. Just keep your feelings open and spend some time with May, and send her love."

"John, it says that I should forgive May," I asked. "How do I do that?"

"I can't really tell you, Tracy. That's just something you have to figure out by yourself. But I know you can do it. Just ask her to forgive you. And, don't forget, you can call me if you need to talk."

I left John's office in a kind of a daze that day. I was already thinking of how to ask May's forgiveness. I hardly felt the rain on my face as I walked to my car. I had forgotten my umbrella.

The whole thing just became too overwhelming for me. Every time I thought about how to ask May's forgiveness, I just was short-circuiting. I mean, she wasn't there, was she? I finally decided to forget about it for a few days. Maybe I was learning something from John, after all.

One evening later that week as I fell asleep I was thinking about May, and how sorry I felt, and I just remember saying in my mind, "Oh May, can you ever forgive me?"

I had a really vivid dream. I dreamt I was in a jumbo jet en route to my appointment in L.A. I was sitting in the middle of the plane, two seats over from the aisle on my right. A really attractive young woman came and sat down in the aisle seat. She glanced at me and arched her eyebrows and wrinkled her nose up like she was asking a question as she sat down. I felt it was a really endearing expression. She was maybe around eighteen, with radiant long blond hair pushed back behind her ears. She was wearing a white top and black pants. She began a conversation with me and we chit-chatted for a while. All along I had this feeling that I knew her, that we had met before somewhere. Throughout the conversation she kept looking me in the eyes, and one time when our eyes met an electric shock went through me. I knew beyond doubt that it was May! I could see that she knew who I was. I guessed she had known the whole time. Then she said to me in her musical voice, "I've just been waiting for you to know me."

"Oh May!" I said, and I reached over and we hugged for a long time. When I released her and sat back, I somehow found the courage to look her in the eye and I asked her, "Oh May, can you possibly find it in your heart to forgive me?" She looked back at me with her beautiful, sunny smile, and answered, "Certainly, Mother, I forgive you for everything. I love you. Thank you for finding me!"

My happiness was extreme. I was laughing and crying at the same time. And we were hugging. Then I looked down to get a tissue from my bag, and when I looked up May was gone. I was left with an unbelievable feeling of warmth and love that was actually a physical sensation like floating in the warm sea, and gently rocking. I looked around for her, but she was gone.

I woke up in my bed with tears on my face, and feeling blessed. When I tried to explain it all to Lewis he just shrugged, and said he was happy for me. That's Lewis for you.

When I called John to tell him the news he was very pleased. He said he had known, I'll never know how, that I had released May. He thought the dream on the jet was extraordinary. "Well, Tracy, you've done it, and in such a beautiful way. I'm so happy for you. You know, that's about it. I've done all I can for you now. Please stay in touch, and call me anytime if you need me."

I called John again about three or four months later to let him know that I was going to have a baby after all. "You'll be sorry, Tracy!" he said and laughed. He was still laughing when I hung up the phone.

A Conversation with John Myerson on Healing from Spiritual Interference and Connecting to the Universe with Love

This interview was conducted by Robert Greenebaum with shamanic healer John Myerson.

RG: John, the subject for today is spiritual interference, as in the story of Tracy. What does it actually mean? What is spiritual interference?

JM: It means that something is getting in the way. "Spiritual interference" is blocking by a "spirit"—another soul, another person, either living or dead who is affecting you, in some adverse way.

RG: Well, what would that be? When you say "getting in the way" what is the interference getting in the way of?

JM: It's getting in the way of either health, or doing something you want to do, or growth. In this case, with Tracy, it was getting in the way of her ability to get pregnant. And, once the interference was resolved, and she made peace with it, she was able to relax, and to flow, and to get pregnant, which was her goal. And I've had other patients with similar problems. For example, I have a patient I talked to recently who is fifty-four years old, and when she was eighteen she had an abortion. She said at that point that she just shut down her reproductive system. She knows she did it herself. She still had her periods, but she never used contraceptives again, and was married twice, and active sexually, but never got pregnant. And she said to me that she knows that she didn't allow herself to get pregnant.

RG: There have been a number of patients that have had a similar problem with an abortion.

JM: Correct. That's the most common. I've also had a few cases that were abortions in a past life, but most of them are abortions in this lifetime.

RG: In that case the spiritual interference is the existence of another soul attached in some way to the person. This is not necessarily malevolent. The interference is that the other soul is there at all—in some way affecting or blocking the person's energy.

JM: Right. And that would be an example of subtle interference—somebody who goes through her life, and everything's fine, except, for instance, she wants to get pregnant and she can't. It's not affecting her all the time. I also see people who have extreme cases of spiritual influence, for instance one woman who was being harmed continually by an ex-boyfriend. This happened during my apprenticeship. Here's the story:

I had known Donna for awhile but had not seen her for some time. She called and said she was in trouble. Donna is the kind of person who when she asks for help, you respond. She came to see me and she did not look good. She is usually vibrant and strong—an athletic woman of Italian ancestry. Now she looked weak and had a dark edge to her aura. She looked like her life force was being drained from her.

This turned out to be the case. She had been seeing a new boyfriend for the past few months. He had become domineering and demanding. Usually, Donna would get rid of him as fast as you can blink. But for some reason, in this case, she could not. She felt there was some karmic connection between them and that he was draining her of energy.

When I looked at him in the shamanic world, I found this to be true. I "saw" at least one lifetime where he was extremely abusive to her. This came to me as a vision. Sort of like watching a video that was clear and full of emotion. I began immediately to try to separate the two of them.

It was not working out. I had tried everything I could think of and she was only getting worse. His health was not good. He had seizures and heart problems but every time he saw her, he would look better for awhile. Donna would look worse.

I called my teacher on the telephone and asked for help. She replied that he was evil. This was a strong word for her to use. Usually she is the kindest, gentlest person, always looking for the good in people. A Christian in the truest sense. However, shamans are trained to work with love for healing and with power to get rid of evil or perceived enemies. This was the case with Donna. My teacher told me to call on Donna's boyfriend's soul at a certain time early the next morning. I was supposed to hold his attention and then she would do the rest. I was very intrigued to say the least.

I did what she asked the next day and held his attention. All of a sudden there seemed to be a crack in the energy field around me and then he just disappeared. I could not find him anywhere. That morning I called my teacher on the phone and asked what happened. She just laughed a little girl laugh and, "Don't worry, he will not bother her anymore. I talked with his soul and convinced him to see things my way. I just scared him a little."

I saw Donna two days later and she did look better. She had not heard from the boyfriend for the past two days. That was unusual since he was calling her at least once per day. I asked her to look into it. She called me back the next day and said that she could not find him at all so she called his brother. Her boyfriend, early in the morning that we had worked on him, had had a minor heart attack and was hospitalized. This was his third heart attack. Coincidence? Donna never heard from him again.

By contrast, what I usually do now is to call the patient's soul to me, and I see the other person attached. I then make a pathway for this attached aspect to go into some other realm. If it goes willingly, like the soul attached to Tracy did, everything is made peaceful. The separation is accomplished without problems. However, in this extreme case, the man was not going. This was evil. We needed to force him to go so he couldn't get back.

RG: Like a permanent banishment.

JM: Yes, that's right. When this is done, the energy builds and builds, like a thunderstorm. Finally the lightning strikes, he is gone, and I shut the door immediately. It's shocking for the other person who is sent away. The patient feels immediately relieved and lighter.

RG: Does the person who is interfering usually know it?

JM: In most cases I would say that they don't. And then I try to be as gentle as possible. I reason with the soul. I have the patient help so that it's a nice break-off with no problems. But in this case—which is an extreme case—Donna's boyfriend knew exactly what he was doing. And what he was doing was evil. It felt evil. I saw nothing good in it, nor in him either. Interestingly enough, he died four or five years later from completely unrelated causes, and he never contacted my patient again. Not even once.

RG: You mentioned, John, that the way that you would usually do this— for instance, what you did with Tracy—is to use a process. In the story she needs to ask for forgiveness, and to take other interim steps. Could you discuss how you would work directly with someone in a case like Tracy, where you were trying to be gentle with the interfering aspect as well as the patient?

JM: I call this process "separation." What I mean by separation is that different souls—different beings—are connected. And when you look at the connections they look like white lines, or filaments, or sometimes roots. Sometimes they're thick, sometimes they're thin. Sometimes they look like a net, or network. Sometimes they look like one big tube. But, whatever, those connections have to be released. The best way to do it is to release them like a root, if you envision that there's a root in the person who needs healing. And the best way to do it is to get the whole root out and let it go, instead of just pulling it off at the top. The way to do this is to use love and forgiveness. So what Tracy was able to do was to forgive herself for having the abortion, and to love the soul that was her aborted child. And when she could do that, the child was satisfied, the spirit was happy and she agreed to leave. So, you can see it's a method of using love and forgiveness for personal growth. And that tends to be my focus in my practice—to use shamanic healing for self-transformation, or growth—changing the consciousness of the person that I'm working with. That's why in this situation with Tracy I had her do a lot of the work, so she could feel the process happening. So she could be a part of the process, and could feel the growth and change in herself. Whereas, in the example with Donna, it just wasn't possible because of the evil in the situation, and the harm that was being done. I had to step in. A traditional shaman steps in, takes action, and then it's over with. By contrast, my general focus is to get people involved in their own healing, in their own growth, in their own changing of consciousness. So, Tracy was able to make a connection with the soul of her aborted child, and when that happened she was able to let go of the trauma associated with it—in her body and her being—and in doing so she healed herself.

RG: Some people would call those connections "heartstrings." Quite often when I've discussed some of these issues with people, they have difficulty with the idea of an actual connection.

JM: The connections are real. They may not be physical, but they are real. I can see them, and their effects.

RG: And there's a root at each end, in each person?

JM: Probably there is a root in the other end. I never thought about that. All I want to do is get it off the person I'm trying to heal.

RG: So it's not the actual connection that you want to release, it's just the end that's in the patient?

JM: Yes.

RG: This release can be a difficult experience for people to go through.

JM: Sometimes it's extremely difficult. It's always emotional. But a lot of it is beautiful—like what happened with Tracy—you know, the feeling of peace and happiness in her was awesome. Usually what happens is they feel the other person, the other soul, fading away. They don't usually go instantly. It's a fading process. One day it's just not there. Either they can actually feel it fading away, or the next time they call on the soul it's not there—there's no longer a connection. It's not there, there's nothing there. But it's usually a fading process.

RG: What about anger associated with this?

JM: Well, a separation has to be done with love. Because it's the anger that is keeping the attachment alive. The anger, the fear, or the anxiety. Until that is dissolved the attachment stays. You could say that the emotion is the attachment.

RG: I'm a little bit confused. You're saying that someone—for instance, if Donna was angry at the ex-boyfriend, that is the attachment. That's what you're saying?

JM: Well, Donna's not a good example, because nothing of this faded. She's an extreme example.

RG: All I'm talking about is her feelings, though.

JM: Right. I understand that. She had all kinds of feelings for him. But, when he was gone they weren't there anymore. But she didn't work through letting go, she couldn't. It was too severe. He was too evil and and too strong for her, and he was starting to take her over, so there was none of that in this case.

RG: Let's talk about Tracy then. She had feelings related to this, but the actual connection was buried under layers and layers of other feelings.

JM: Correct. But once she forgave herself for having the abortion, and let go of her anger towards herself for having the abortion, and made peace with herself and her aborted child, she was able to let the whole thing go. In other words she let go of her anger, and there might have been some fear too.

RG: What I'm trying to talk about here is the fact that someone may not know that he or she has a spiritual interference, or an unhealthy inter-personal attachment. They may just feel angry about things in general.

And they may come to see you because they have these strong feelings, and they would just like some help "getting out of them."

JM: Most of the people who come to me are that way. Tracy's need was to get pregnant. Donna's need was to deal with evil. But most people come because they are angry all the time, or they are fearful all the time. Or they are angry and fearful. Or they find that at work they are just exploding at people with anger. Or, they can't get along with the opposite sex at all. Or the same sex.

RG: Or they might be sad all the time. It doesn't have to be angry.

JM: Absolutely. They could be sad all the time. Or they could be depressed—very depressed. And what I do is, I just start searching. I just start searching with them to see what's there.

RG: What the root cause of the feeling is?

JM: Right. There can be many causes. It can be parents, siblings, husbands, wives, boyfriends, girlfriends, workers, friends, relatives—anything. I just sort of go down the list and see where it is. And some people have lots of stuff that's happened in their lives, so there's more than one person they need to work on releasing.

RG: John, since you are a psychologist, and some of these patients may be coming for psychotherapy, what is the difference between your approach to this kind of a problem and conventional psychotherapy?

JM: I try to get them to live the emotions. It's beyond feeling them. I don't want them to just talk about them. I want them to actually experience them with me. So, for example, if I were doing a dream interpretation, I don't do an interpretation of what's happening. Much more importantly, a strong dream is a portal or a gateway leading into something else. So, I have the patient re-enter the dream, and the two of us go into the dream together and re-experience it. From there I find out where the situation needs to move. And, the same is true with any experience. For instance, I have a woman with an abusive father, and we go back together and relive those situations where the child was abused. And not just talking about it. We would actually relive it. And then we would do a separation with the father's soul. We try to release it. It's a very emotional process. It's not something we sit and clinically talk about. It actually is much, much deeper than that. I've had people, for example, who have done inner child work—which is basically going back and feeling what you were like when you were a child, to see if you can help the "child" within—people who have done a lot of that work, and then do it again with me, realize that it's a different process—because it's deeper. It has more emotional content to it. And I am able to go there with the person. So, if they have memories of childhood and they describe them to me, we actually become that vision. We know we can't change the past, but if you can change your perception of the past, you effectively change the present.

RG: It sounds like in some way there is—along the concept of the Akashic records—a place where this actual, let's say, in this case, an abuse incident, still exists. And that you can actually go there with the patient, and help them through it again.

JM: Correct. And you can't change it. It's still going to be in the records, but you can change your relationship to it. So, like Tracy was able to separate from the aborted soul, you can separate from the memory or the vision of the abuse—which doesn't negate that it happened, it just releases the emotional constellation that you're carrying around with you.

RG: It sounds like Freudian catharsis to me.

JM: Right. Except that you actually live it. My personal opinion is that Freudian analysts, and Jungian work, and cognitive therapists, all do a part of this. This to me is the whole of it.

RG: So, for you, personally, when you go into one of these events with a patient it's real for you.

JM: Very real! I have to live it too.

RG: Now, do you live it the way they lived it, or do you live it the way you live it?

JM: No, I live it the way I live it. I can feel the way they lived it, but if I'm to help them I have to be able to be there for them. So it's more like if you bring home a friend for dinner, and then you get in a fight with your mother, and the friend is watching. It's more like I'm there with them, but not "in it."

RG: And in some cases, from what you've told me in the past, this might have to be done over a period of time, and repeated until it's over.

JM: Sometimes many times.

RG: So there's a challenge for someone who comes to you whether they can stick with you through the therapeutic process.

JM: It's a very difficult process and it takes a lot of courage to do it. It's not easy. My heart always goes out to those who can do it! It can be very frightening, but very rewarding in the end.

RG: That brings up an issue for me. If someone is mildly irritated all the time, they might not ever come to you.

JM: Correct. Usually when they come to me, people have a "big thing." It gets to the place where the pain and suffering of living with it is much worse than blocking it.

RG: As an analogy, you have an infected wound, and you need to clean it out. And at that point you can't not clean it out. If you're going to heal from it, you have to go through the process, however painful it is of cleaning out the wound and healing.

JM: There's a wound. But the wound is not physical.

RG: Tracy had a problem that originated from an event that happened quite a while ago, which had become buried. That memory, or the energy involved in the events which that memory was related to, was somehow blocking her from going in the direction that she wanted to go. What was she remembering? She didn't remember it, but somehow there was a memory there, that you had to work with her to uncover and make accessible to her. It wasn't accessible originally. And part of your process with her was to help her to remember that, and not only to remember it, but to go way inside. What I'd like to know is, how do you feel about memories in general, and particularly these buried memories?

JM: A memory of an event that happened five minutes ago is going to be different than a memory of an event that happened thirty years ago. But regardless, memories, like thoughts, have energy, and their energy will continue to affect you, no matter how long ago the event occurred. Whether you've forgotten the memory, or not forgotten the memory, is inconsequential.

Sometimes I can sense what's going on. Other times I ask questions based on experience. And, in this kind of case, where it's related to fertility, one of the questions is, "Was there an abortion?" In Tracy's case I could sense it beforehand. However, I would ordinarily ask that question anyway. And a practitioner such as myself, or any therapist, would ask many questions to see what the reaction is going to be. And if you get a certain reaction then you would probe a little deeper.

RG: Do you think people are made up of their memories?

JM: To a certain extent, yes. I would say that whatever experiences we have—and our memories of those experiences—color the way we act and make choices in everyday life today. You know, people say that living is based on experience, but what's an experience? It's a memory of something happening.

RG: If someone has a memory that is in some way unhealthy—it's blocked—what does it mean for the memory to be blocked, or covered up? They forgot it?

JM: Somehow the memory will affect you negatively, if it's a "bad" memory—just like a good memory will affect you positively. And, you know, having a bad memory of your ice cream cone falling into the street, and you losing your ice cream cone when you were seven, is a bad memory, but not one that's going to create conflict in you when you're thirty-five. However, a memory of having an abortion is a different story, and that creates a whole complex of emotions, a group of emotions, that is traumatic, that has more than one emotion to it. It's got lots of stuff around it. And, it sort of sits like something blocking the train track, or a kink in your water hose. And, you know, sometimes it just blocks everything from happening. Eventually your thoughts get translated into something that's physical, i.e., something that doesn't work as it should. Now, Tracy had her periods, and she ovulated, and everything else, but somehow that didn't matter. She still wasn't able to get pregnant. So, something in her psyche was still holding onto that memory of the abortion, and was not allowing her to get pregnant.

RG: People sometimes say, "My demons are acting up today." And this sounds similar to me—that this kind of a complex or constellation that you're talking about, can have a life of its own.

JM: That's right.

RG: Almost like an animate being.

JM: I absolutely agree with you.

RG: Are we still talking about memory here?

JM: Well, it grows into something bigger than just the thought of it. Especially if it's something as complex and as disturbing as having an abortion was for Tracy.

RG: It takes on a life of its own.

JM: That's right. For example, the patient who told me that she stopped herself from getting pregnant again. She never used contraceptives again, and never got pregnant. I found it very fascinating that this would be volunteered, but it's based on exactly what it is we're talking about.

RG: It sounds different to me because that's conscious.

JM: Well, I don't think she consciously did it, I just think she consciously understood what was going on. She could somehow feel that complex, that constellation of emotions that were in her, and she was just going to leave them there. She was going to leave them in place and block it so she wouldn't get pregnant again.

RG: Oh, I see what you're saying. Well, a memory can be emotional. But memory and emotion are not the same thing. So when you're talking about this complex of emotions...

JM: They belong to an event.

RG: They're associated with it?

JM: Right, and sometimes they go so deep that the person can't remember them at all. I've had people who I've asked, "Have you had an abortion?" and they've said, "No." It turns out they have. Or, like people who have been molested sexually and don't remember it at all. They've blocked the experience. Or if they've been beaten as children. You know, one of the defense mechanisms for getting over that—for surviving in your life—is to bury it so deep that it's "not there anymore." You can't even remember it at all. It's kind of scary when you think about it.

RG: It is kind of scary. What do you think it's buried in?

JM: The same place this was. Somehow in your body-mind. By that I definitely mean it can be buried anywhere. You know, physically, or emotionally. In Tracy's case what I did was to release it emotionally and psychically, and that affected her physically, so she was able to get pregnant.

RG: I don't understand how that can happen.

JM: I don't either. I absolutely agree with you. I have no idea. Scientifically, I have no idea how it happens. All I know is that it does.

RG: What about unscientifically? What do you experience when you see that change in a person?

JM: It's like a rush of energy. It feels like there's been a release. Or, sometimes it feels like there's light in the area, or light around the person where there wasn't before. It's always an emotional change.

RG: The person has "brightened up?"

JM: Every therapist knows this. Every psychotherapist has seen this. Body-centered psychotherapists work on this all the time. That's all they work on is to get a somatic release that affects the emotions. I work on it the other way around. I try to get the emotional release that affects the body. It's what Bernie Siegel was talking about in "Healing with Love." You know, healing the body with true love. He's talking about emotion that's going to affect cancer. You know this is not new. This has been around since man started. The exact mechanism, however, is not known. As far as I know, anyway.

RG: Well, there is a distinction between the inner world and the outer world. Now the body is definitely in the outer world, although the feelings, and probably the emotions and the memories are at least partially in the inner world.

JM: Right. But one affects the other. The point being that you are—that's why I call it the body-mind, the body, mind, spirit—you know, you, the entity, are more than just the physical being sitting in front of me.

RG: What is the "more"?

JM: More is the mind and the spirit.

RG: I know a number of people who don't believe that there is any such thing as a spirit or soul.

JM: Yeah. But, you know, then you have to ask, "What is life?" You know, you have a bunch of chemicals sitting in front of me, but ninety-five to ninety-eight percent of it is water, and you have some bones, and you've got a couple of other things going on there. Why are you alive? There's something to it—that makes you unique from the couch that you're sitting on. And, to me it's an energy, a spirit, that is present in everything that's living. Can I prove that? No. That's just my feeling.

RG: It appears that what you do is deal with the flow of the person's life. You're dealing directly with that. You're dealing with the whole person, but somehow you go way deep inside and deal with the actual flow of their life, like changing the course of a stream or a river by removing an obstacle.

JM: You see, I don't really change the course, but I agree with the analogy. I would go into the river and remove the blockage that's impeding the flow. But changing the actual course of the river is a different story. But I agree with you that there's a flow to everything, there's a flow to life like the river is a flow, and sometimes you get beaver dams, and sometimes you get rocks in the way and sometimes sediment builds up, and who knows what else.

RG: And some of that stuff is natural, and it's part of the person's life willy-nilly. I mean, it's not something that you can change. For instance, if the woman does have an abortion—to stick with the story for a minute—and by an unfortunate circumstance it permanently affects her ability to have children, she can't. So, that changes the landscape, so the "river" would flow a different way. That's what I meant.

JM: No question, I agree.

RG: But if the "river" is only blocked, and there are two possible paths, then you can open that up. So you're going way deep inside the person's actual life...

JM: ...flow.

RG: ...the flow of the person's life. So, how do you experience that "life flow?"

JM: I feel it as an energy. You know, I can feel it on my body. I can feel it as thoughts and as a pattern.

RG: Is that a direct experience for you?

JM: It's a direct experience for me. And, you know, we've all had this kind of thing where, say, for example, you're sitting out by the ocean watching the waves coming in and you're getting this energy, this flow of nature where you can actually feel what's going on out there. You get into a "nature experience." You can have it in the woods, you can have it at the beach—I mean, anywhere outside—and it's very common. I do that with a person. So, instead of nature, I'm experiencing the person in that way.

RG: And that allows you to find out where this obstacle might be.

JM: Correct.

RG: Could you give an example in relation to Tracy about how you experienced her, and how the obstacle seemed to you?

JM: When I met Tracy she was emotionally distraught, she was extremely tense—very wound-up. The image that came to me was a little girl curled up in a corner, and she couldn't get out. I tried to relax her in the beginning. I tried to get to know her a little bit. That's why I used acupuncture. That's why we talked—to establish some kind of connection, to go on together. Because, quite simply, when she came in I couldn't feel anything, except all her distress, and the emotional constellation about not being pregnant. About not feeling good enough about herself. About failing in her role as a woman to have a child. Now, I knew that wasn't preventing her from getting pregnant; however, that can certainly contribute to it. So, the idea for me in the beginning was to basically relax her around those issues. Take the pressure off. Get her to back up. Get her to slow down. Get her just to be Tracy again. And then we'll see.

Once I did that I could feel that something wasn't right. And, what came to me—if you can put yourself in a quiet enough place when you feel these things, sometimes you get flashes, sort of like a *déjà vu* kind of flash. Or sometimes, you know, when the phone rings you just get a flash that you know who it is. Or like Isaac Newton sitting under the tree, and seeing an apple fall—boom, all of a sudden he got an idea of how to do these things. And this is what happens to me. I just wait. And I wait for something to tell me. I get some kind of insight into what happens. And that's when I could see—I saw a baby around her. So that's why I asked her whether she had an abortion.

RG: When you said you saw a "baby around her," what do you mean by "around"?

JM: Well, I saw it up above her head. To my left, her right. And, obviously, I didn't "see" it with my eyes. But, I see it with what is called the "third eye." It's like a waking daydream, I guess you'd call it.

RG: People used to call this "the second sight"?

JM: Correct. What that is I don't know. But, it's an intuition I feel and see at the same time.

RG: And this was a strong one?

JM: Whenever it's strong, I always go with it because I trust it. Over the years it's been correct. Sometimes you get weak ones. And sometimes you get ones you can't pick up at all. So you just have to wait.

RG: Let me go back for just a second here. You said "until she could become Tracy again." She was so distressed that she had forgotten who she was?

JM: Well, you know, she had changed. She was becoming a workaholic; she was not having a relationship with her husband; she was not happy; all those kinds of things. As I said, the emotions were incredibly strong, especially the one about being a failure as a woman having a child.

RG: Part of the process that she has to go through is to remember who she is.

JM: In some cases people can get themselves worked up. So, say there really is nothing wrong with Tracy. And, say she never had an abortion, and all that happened was the first couple of months she tried to get pregnant she didn't, just by chance. It just didn't happen that month. And she could start to get worried about it. And the next month if it didn't happen she's getting even more worried. And this is going on and on and on. And there really is nothing wrong with her, except that she's now created a situation where she can't get pregnant because she's made herself too emotionally upset. So, in those cases all that you do is to calm the person down again—just the acupuncture helps. You can use herbs to help. You can talk to her to help. And in that case, when you calm her down, then the person can get pregnant again. So, I've seen that too. That's not shamanic healing, that's Oriental medicine. Or psychotherapy. Or a combination of Oriental medicine and psycho-therapy.

RG: It sounds like she's starting to create one of those complexes that you were talking about a minute ago.

JM: Absolutely. She's creating it, and we're just catching it real early. No question. No question about that.

RG: Well, it seems to me that she's in the process of forgetting who she was before it all started.

JM: OK. I'll agree with you there.

RG: You basically wipe what are at that point very thin layers off, to get her back to where she was before the current problems started.

JM: I would agree with that.

RG: And then, going beyond that, it sounds like what you do is you continue that process further and further and further inside, until you reach that kernel of whatever it is that's causing the problem.

JM: Correct. And some people when you get there, there is no kernel. And so you know there is no problem, and you've solved it. And, to follow this example, they'll just get pregnant. But with Tracy, what came to me was, there was a kernel—a big one.

RG: If just talking about something and helping to calm her down is not what you are calling "shamanic healing", at some point it does change over. When you start basing it on your deeper and deeper and deeper intuition, and you're relating deeper and deeper to her, then you are entering a different area.

JM: I agree with that.

RG: Can you feel when that happens?

JM: Absolutely. I call it a connection. It's a feeling of being able to feel her "flow," being able to immerse myself in the river that's her flow. When that happens then it's made that cross-over. And I try to do that with everybody anyway, no matter what happens. That's how I know for sure where we are.

RG: Since you've done this with many people, is it pretty easy? Or is it still hard for you?

JM: I do it naturally, because I do it so much.

RG: But at some point you learned to do this.

JM: That's what learning the craft is all about. I think I had the ability to do it anyway, and I think that when you have patients as an Oriental medical practitioner—all practitioners of any healing art have that to a certain extent—and then I just increased it in my training in shamanic healing.

RG: "Just increased it," to some people would seem pretty amazing.

JM: I've worked on this for many years. It didn't happen yesterday. You know, I've been in practice for twenty-five years. I've practiced this every single day. You know, I'm at work for six to eight hours every day, so I'm practicing it there, and I practice it when I do all my other practices. So, I work on this constantly. You're right—I did say "just," but it's more than just that.

RG: Can you access your intuition by will?

J; Yes.

RG: And what is that like?

JM: I guess I call it a process of letting go, to use a Buddhist term. It happens when you calm your mind, and when your mind starts to expand. It feels like the expanding of your mind, when your thoughts cease. That's how it happens.

RG: Your thoughts cease, and then what happens?

JM: Well, what happens in meditation is that it's a process whereby you learn that you and your thoughts are not the same. So, when you meditate, you try to trick your mind into focusing on something that's not your thoughts. In most cases it's on your breath, or a mantra, or a vision. And what happens there—obviously your mind keeps wandering back to your thoughts, back and forth—and eventually you get to a place where you realize your thoughts have faded into the background, and your mind seems to expand and become very clear. And that to me is the gateway. That is the place I go—I use—to get into these other places. And you can train yourself to do that.

RG: And once you get to that place where the intuition is accessible to you, what do you experience at that point?

JM: Well. To me it's a gateway into what I call "the other realms," into the shamanic realms. And those are unlimited. Sometimes I go places. Other times I just sit and wait. Other times I contact the soul, or the spirit, of the person who's in front of me, that I'm dealing with, so that I can get those insights. And I do that just by sitting here.

RG: Many people say that they would have an insight, or they could be intuitive about something. For instance, an EMT must just act. And I would say they would be accessing intuition—that would be a different kind of intuition. Or, in a less emergency-related situation, a researcher who had studied a subject for years would start to have insights about the way to do the research.

JM: Absolutely, and when you read the accounts of scientists who did that—for example, the famous story about Archimedes in his bathtub.

RG: What's the bathtub story?

JM: Archimedes was relaxing in his bath, and boom, there came the insight about buoyancy, after which he ran through the streets exclaiming, "Eureka!" So, you say, "Well, where'd that come from?" It came from somewhere. Whatever you call "where it came from", that's what I try to use.

RG: Well, what do some people call "where it came from"? What are some possible names for that?

JM: Well, the first name was "intuition". It's just that your mind makes a leap when you let it relax, it's all logical. That's fine. But to me it's more than that. To me it is letting your mind relax, but it's also receiving energy, receiving imprints and information that I have no way of knowing. I mean, how did I know Tracy had an abortion? You might say that based on experience I'd ask the question, but why did I ask it that day? I asked it that day because I could see it. If she had walked in the door here the first day, and I had said, "Well, have you had an abortion?" it wouldn't have worked at all. She was in too much of an emotional state of her own to be able to access the hidden memory. That's why I wait until I can see something, and I know it's right. That's when I act on it.

RG: Do you think the person is actually sending you some information, through the other realm?

JM: Sure. Absolutely.

RG: The patient is actually sending you a message non-verbally.

JM: Correct. Either the person or the spirit of the aborted soul that's tied to her—is sending it to me.

RG: Is that telepathy?

JM: Telepathy is with people who are alive, yes?—knowing what they think. I'm not sure this was telepathy, because I wasn't getting anything cognitive from her.

RG: What do you mean by "cognitive"?

JM: Well telepathy, as I understand it, is being able to hear your thoughts. Now, I'm not sure I can hear your thoughts. I don't know what you're thinking right now. Sometimes I can feel your emotions, I can feel what you're feeling. But this—I wasn't feeling what she was feeling—I was "seeing" something around her.

RG: If she was sending you something, it was something related to the memory constellation we discussed earlier.

JM: And, as I said, I'm not sure she was sending me the memory. It could have been the spirit of the aborted soul—the baby could have been sending it to me also.

RG: Or other beings?

JM: Or other beings, possibly, too.

RG: It was like a…

JM: Well, ask yourself, "Why didn't I see it from the beginning?" If that soul was there why didn't I see it when she walked in the door weeks beforehand? I don't know why. But that was the first time I saw it. That's how I knew it was time to bring it up.

RG: Let's talk about what happens with her as she goes through the process. When she starts out, she's very distressed. You calm her down. You talk a little bit with her in the context of a normal relationship. And then you get your intuition. During this time her attitudes are changing. She was originally frenzied, and now she's in normal consciousness. And then it sounds like what you would do is to probe some more to find out for yourself where you think this should move.

JM: In this case, there was no more research. It was just—BOOM!—I saw the soul, I asked her the question. Sometimes that is the case. I go back and I contact the spirit, and I say, "What do you want? What's going on?" Or, I'll see it when the person's not even here. And then I'll think about what it is, and feel and then go back and ask her. So, sometimes that is absolutely the case. In this particular case that wasn't so. You know, I saw the soul, and I asked her right away. Because I was so sure what it was. Now, if she had said, "No. I never had an abortion." I would have contacted that, and seen what it was.

RG: Would you have talked with her some more, trying to experience...?

JM: Yes.

RG: ...that at the same time?

JM: Absolutely. And while she isn't here.

RG: At that point you have to decide how you're going to treat this now.

JM: Sometimes I think about it, and sometimes I just do it. It depends, again, on what feels right.

RG: You brought this into her consciousness, by asking her. She wasn't aware of it—she didn't remember it—until you asked her. Then she started also remembering and re-experiencing some of the emotions that she had blocked.

JM: When she's ready to hear this, it triggers something in her. It opens a door that's been shut. And once the door's open, you can't shut it again. And so, for her, the memories start to flow. She's going to start to feel it, because I opened that door for her. So, it's like I somehow reached into the flow, and just sort of touched the blockage somehow.

RG: Or turned the key...

JM: Turned the key, opened the door, lifted the veil—whatever expression you want to use. And once that happens then you can't go back again.

RG: What would have happened to her if she didn't see you anymore at that point?

JM: Well, two things. Either she would have had the memories on her own and eventually gotten better. Or, she would have built another wall around the blockage. It would have hurt for a while, emotionally, and then she just would have built a scar up over it—which would have made it even harder to access. But I was able to keep it open. Keep it open, keep it open, keep it open—keep her experiencing it, keep her experiencing it—until she was right there with it too.

RG: I just want to clarify this. You said you can't shut the door again...

JM: But you can build another wall...

RG: ...you can build another wall that would make a new door.

JM: But that's hard to do.

RG: But that didn't happen. She stayed with the therapy. Then you took her through what is essentially the core healing process. The story discusses that from her point of view, but let's talk about it from your point of view.

JM: I get her to make contact with the baby—the soul. I get her to do that by naming it. I ask her to decide whether it's a boy or a girl. Well, to decide that you have to feel it. Then I ask her to name it. I ask her to do that so it becomes personal. Now it's not just some abortion she had, now it's a girl named whatever. So this is now real. This is now personal. And then I ask her to establish more contact with it, by talking to it—in this case her. And I do that to get her back into the whole complex, and stay there. In this case it was a beautiful dream of being on an airplane and meeting her—that's how she released it. She had a vision, and then once that happens, the blockage, the emotion, the energy associated with it is gone.

RG: Tracy had a relationship with the aborted soul. In other words, Tracy's soul had a relationship with the aborted soul. We're talking about souls now. To some people that's a difficult concept, so before we go any further on relationships can we discuss that a little bit?

JM: Well you know, it's interesting. When I got into this area I always thought that this was the strangest thing in the world, but it seems to have been around since day one with people. And, surprisingly enough, people are never surprised when I talk about it—very rarely. You know, people always tell me that they talk to their dear departed father, or mother, or spouse, or friend, or—I mean, it's amazing—people tell me this, I mean all the time, and unsolicited. So I think the concept that when people die they're not necessarily gone is not a new one. Whether you believe the soul is actually there, as an entity, or whether it's just in somebody's imagination and they're making it up in their heads to make themselves feel better—I couldn't answer that for you. But feeling and talking and being with whatever you want to call something that has died and moved on—I call it a soul—is not unusual. And usually when I bring it up to people, ninety-nine percent of the time I never get a weird reaction, no matter who they are or where they come from. Every now and then I will, and that's unusual.

RG: You also talk and deal with souls of the living. That is a harder concept for people than souls of the dead.

JM: I would agree with that. I absolutely agree with you.

RG: We were talking before that there's a spirit, there's some kind of a life force that is different from rocks and stones and bones and flesh—that is a life flow, I think is what we said. Now, is that the soul?

JM: I'm not sure what it is. I don't sit and analyze it. I don't make a theoretical model for people. I don't ever question what it is, or why, or anything like that. All I know is whatever it is, I can contact it. And when I can contact it I can feel it. I can get information from it. I can do whatever. And that's all I care about. So, I tend to be very practical, and very pragmatic. And whether it's the soul, or whether it's a spirit, or whether it's the life-force—I only use those words when I'm trying to convey to somebody else what it is I'm actually doing. But to me the doing is the most important thing—the feeling, the connection, the actual experience of what it is that we're doing. The relationship that you have with it is the most important thing to me. And, you know, I've debated with people whether it's real, or whether it's in my head, or whether it's a dream, or it's all made up, or whether it's a psychotic break, or—to me I don't care. All I know is that it works, I can do it, and I can help other people do it, and things happen when you "can do it." So, when you have that relationship with the soul, that somehow you and it merge, talk, feel—anything like that—something always happens.

RG: You're talking about the other person's soul. Do you feel that your soul is talking to the other person's soul, and that you are able to apprehend this in some way?

JM: Right. Or my being, my body-mind-spirit, is able to connect on some level with his or her body-mind-spirit, whatever form that's taking.

RG: You would consider it an expanded definition of what a person is.

JM: That's right. Into other realms. Absolutely. And the experience can happen on any of those realms. In other words you can experience another person physically—you can touch them. You can feel a sensation on your body from them. You can have a mind-to-mind connection when you know what they're thinking or you see or feel or get information that's coming from them.

RG: I think many people would consider the story of Tracy's healing from her abortion, and then being able to get pregnant, to be a miracle. You know that we're talking about some edgy concepts for people. Souls, spirits, body-minds, healing, and what seem to be miraculous results. Now, I know that you don't present yourself as a religious miracle-maker in the old style. And as you said a moment ago, you're very pragmatic about this. But to some people this would seem to be a miracle. How do you feel about that?

JM: You see, to me it's so real, in that I experience it every day, that's it's not a miracle in the least bit. It's very logical, practical, and pragmatic as much as you and I are sitting here talking. And so, because of that, I don't think of it as strange. I don't think of it as miraculous. It's just something that I can perceive. It is all very real.

RG: I think of a miracle as an event with a beneficial result, that was completely inexplicable, and seemingly impossible.

JM: I think it also is something that happens outside of somebody's experience. So, in other words, for those who not used to working in this area, what happened to Tracy is miraculous. It cant't be explained; it can't be felt; it can't be seen. That person has no idea what happened. To me it's what I do everyday, so it's not miraculous to me. I'm always happy when things like this happen, but I'm not surprised, because I've done it before. In the beginning, was I?—no question. (laughs) Absolutely. I thought it was the most absurd thing I'd ever seen. I felt that with acupuncture, too. The first time I started using acupuncture I thought, "You mean you stick little needles in some-place, and some-thing happens? You gotta be kidding me!" (laughs again) But, my experience tells me it works, because I've done it. So I think it all depends on what your experience is, and where you come from.

RG: I guess what you're saying is that to an isolated, primitive society our technology would seem miraculous. Something similar to that.

JM: Right. And to us it's ordinary. You know, putting a man on the moon. The Internet! Tell me the Internet is not miraculous. You type on your computer, press a button, and somebody else gets a message. That's not miraculous? Well, you know, we're used to it. We do it every day. We do it millions of times. How many people actually know what's going on? Not me!

RG: But you do it without the computer.

JM: But I'm just saying that's miraculous to me. So, it's just a question of your point of view. Think about the tribes in wherever, and the white men sail up with this armada with three-masted ships and cannons, and get out. Tell me that's not miraculous. It seems pretty miraculous. It's interesting. I was giving a talk once at a church in on this topic, and we were talking about healing. It was a men's breakfast. And there were probably fifty or sixty people there. It was a lot of fun. And after I spoke someone got up and said that he came from rural North Carolina. He explained that they didn't have any doctors. When people got sick they all got together and prayed. And, he said, it sounds just like what you do. And he was right. It's very similar to what I do. (laughs) You know, they all got together, they all built up some energy, and they all tried to direct it at the person who needed healing. I just call it "the souls," that's all. They call it angels, or God, or I don't know—whatever you want to call it. To me it's all the same.

RG: For you—and I'm just summarizing here—it's natural. What someone would consider to be supernatural to you is natural. It's a matter of your range of experience, and their range of experience. It's not necessarily "a higher level," it's just more encompassing.

JM: Right. I don't talk about higher levels, or lower levels, or any kind of levels. Everybody has their own consciousness, and everybody's experience lends them to do different things. That's all.

RG: We've established that this is a process. Some parts of it are physical. Some parts are psychological. Some parts are emotional. And some parts go beyond even being emotional, to the spiritual.

JM: And usually, from my perspective, healing happens from the subtle to the gross, i.e., from the spiritual to the physical. Now, other people would disagree with me, and would like to heal the other way around. But that's how I generally work. I try to work from the spiritual to the physical.

RG: That's for the depth part of it. Because you also were using the physical to relax Tracy.

JM: Right. But my ultimate goal was to get something spiritual.

RG: You have Tracy go through a process. And as we were saying, it goes from exterior to interior. From your point of view is it always interior? In other words, you're always trying to have the interior—her deep body-mind—reveal itself.

JM: Yes, that's my goal. And in some people, they walk in here and, "Bingo!" they're already there. They've already done a lot of work. They've done the therapy part. They've done the physical part. They're ready to take another leap, and they find me, and they come in, and that's what we do. Bingo! Right away. Tracy was not like that. She had to go through the whole process with me because she hadn't done anything before. So, for me, it's more work. I need to spend the time. Getting her to relax. Getting her to feel. Talking to her. Making the connection. The whole thing. If someone walks in here and instantly we can make a connection, then we can go. To me, that's, of course, preferable. It would have taken a lot less time than it took with Tracy. And that's not to put Tracy down. I'm just saying that everybody's where they are. And I needed to move her from where she was to another place, so she could heal. And that was the process. Sometimes people come to me already having made the move. They're right there on the edge of the precipice. They just need to jump.

RG: There are multiple relationships involved in which you are trying to make changes with her. In her relationship with herself. In her relationship with her aborted baby. In her relationship with you. And then her overall relationship with a "higher power."

JM: And ultimately her relationship to the universe.

RG: So there are a lot of relationship issues involved, and you also talk about "connections." And you ultimately are talking about separating from the experience of the abortion, and from the aborted soul. Let's talk about what a relationship is for a few minutes. Many people would consider a relationship to be how you relate to somebody else. Or, how you see them, how you interact with them. What I'm interested in is—you have to establish a relationship with the person from zero. You establish a relationship, and in developing your own relationship you find out how they relate—what their style of relating is—and that can give you a clue as to what some of their other relationships are.

JM: Right. And what I try to do with everybody is, I try to just open myself up to them. And by that I mean I just try to be in my heart. I try to be as loving and as compassionate as I can. And usually that will establish a relationship with someone. I mean, someone who's trying to beat you—you're not going to establish a relationship with that person. Someone who's angry at you—you're not going to establish that kind of relationship. Someone who's warm and open and trying to be there with you and for you—you're more likely to come closer to them. So that's what I do in the beginning. And I do that all the time, anyway, but that's what I try to do. And where that takes us I never know, but I'm always interested in waiting to see. And that's the relationship that I try to get—that feeling from my heart—the heart-feeling back and forth.

RG: I guess I was using "relationship" in a more neutral way, because you can have a bad relationship. Some of the abusive types of situations—there's definitely a relationship there. I just want to try to refine the concept a little bit more.

JM: In all relationships, though, there's an exchange of energy. Between two people, or between a person and his or her environment. There are connections on this body-mind-spirit continuum that are not just physical. Besides the body—the physical, touching connection—there's the mind connection, there may be an emotional connection, and there's also a spiritual connection. And I try to establish any kind of connection I can along that continuum. So, if I meet someone I might talk about whatever that person is interested in, whether it's sports, or skiing, or babies, or whatever. From that I try to get into an emotional connection. And from that I try to take it into a spiritual connection. But I try somehow to find a common ground, a common thing, or whatever it is that person wants to talk about, and I use that as an entryway to get him or her into the body-mind-spirit.

RG: Tracy already has all her other relationships and connections before she comes to see you. And part of your process is to identify an unhealthy connection that she has—unhealthy for her. So, somehow you have to sense her relationships, with other people particularly.

JM: As I said, I couldn't see any of that in the beginning, because she was so emotionally distraught and closed that my initial intent was just to establish anything with her. You know, on any level she wanted to talk about, until we could get that emotional craziness around her to calm down. When she walked in the door I couldn't see the aborted soul. Sometimes I can right away, and they're not ready to hear me so I wait, but with her I couldn't see anything. It was just like being inundated with energy coming at you. Like walking out of a cave into bright noontime sunlight—you know, BOOM! All of a sudden you're inundated with too much. And that's what I felt with her when I first met her. So, I couldn't do a whole lot, because I couldn't feel anything. It was a process of getting used to her energy, and getting her to a place where the two of us could have a relationship. And, in truth, she wanted to trust somebody. You know, she needed to talk to somebody. She needed just somebody to be there for her. And that's what I did in the beginning. I didn't judge her. I didn't tell her she was bad. I didn't tell her she was evil. I didn't tell her she had failed the world because she couldn't have a baby. I just was here. And I think that's when the relationship began.

RG: And then it progressed from the physical relaxation, to her opening up to you, finally the story about her abortion, and that's when the real healing process started.

JM: To me that's true.

RG: Her attitude now has changed a lot already. Her attitude towards her own problem—let's just deal with that one—has changed a lot. She's gotten to the point where she's trusting that you're going to help her get through this.

JM: Well, she's also forgotten about the fact that she can't have babies. I mean, not really forgotten about it, but she's not taking her temperature anymore, and she's not researching having in vitro, and everything else. And she's not thinking of taking drugs to help with fertilization. None of that stuff. So, she's dropped all that. She's having sex with her husband when she wants to have sex with her husband. I've distracted her from that, into now thinking about something else, which is the aborted soul.

RG: As you mentioned, she was not able to relate to her abortion the first time you saw her. Later she could, because you gave her experiences of deep feeling.

JM: And she was able to experience those feelings, and it was OK.

RG: Because of your nonjudgmental and respectful attitude towards her.

JM: And plus, I like emotions. So I look for them in here. Whereas most times when you're talking to people they don't want to hear about your emotions. You meet someone on the street, they say, "Hey, how're you doin'?" If you say, "Hey, I'm terrible," they're gone. (laughs) You know, they don't want to hear about it. Emotions are too loaded.

RG: Her attitude is changed. And now, once the subject of her abortion has come up, she initially feels surprised, and then she realizes, no, she's not that surprised. Because she had forgotten about it. And, once you asked her about it, it came back to her.

JM: The memories started flooding back.

RG: You dealt with that for a while, but then you started to initiate a definite process of changing her relationship with the abortion experience—and the aborted soul.

123

JM: Right. I wanted to get it to a spiritual level. So we've taken her from the physical, to the mental—you know, where she thought about it—and then to the emotional, where she was actually feeling the emotions that happened during this experience. And then I wanted to take it a step beyond that, for her to actually connect—as I connect—to the aborted soul, to that soul directly, and talk to it. And that's when I gave the idea of whether it was a boy or a girl. And giving it a name makes it real. And then the separation idea of talking to it and just sharing your story with it, and it will share it with you. So the two of you can make peace with the situation, and it will move on. And this case was beautiful in the dream.

RG: Now we're talking about a separation process.

JM: I want you to see that there's a flow to this whole thing. It moves from the physical, through the mind, into the emotional part, and that's where most people stop it—at the emotional part. And in my mind, until we get it to the spiritual place, until we can release the soul in a spiritual place, healing doesn't happen. Based on my experience, and based on my method of healing, this is what I need to get someone to do.

RG: How do you distinguish the shamanic aspect from the traditional psychotherapy approach?

JM: Well, as soon as we get into the spiritual it becomes shamanic, in my opinion. Up to that point it's not shamanic. The shamanic part for me, of course, was to see it. The diagnosis was shamanic. I saw the aborted soul. I didn't guess that. I could see it. So, that to me is shamanic. Now, to get her to heal shamanically is a different story. What a traditional shaman would have done in the village back in Africa would have been to go into a ritual, where the shaman would experience the healing realms. The patient would lie there and know what the purpose of this is—to release the aborted soul. But the shaman would do it for her. And the ritual would take place, and the person would feel healed because she had a ritual. And the shaman would talk to the soul for the person and release the soul. However, I like to get the person involved. I try to get each person involved in his or her own healing, because I feel that it not only helps them to heal, but it helps change who they are in their relationship to the universe forever. So, in this case that is what I tried to do. There are other cases, like I mentioned before, when that can't be done, because there's danger involved. But, in general, that's what I try to do for most people—to get them involved in what's going on. In this case there was no harm being done. In other words, the aborted soul was not hurting her, she just couldn't get pregnant. And, in order to get pregnant, she had to release it. But there were no health issues.

RG: You're saying if you had wanted to, you could have released it.

JM: Oh, absolutely.

RG: You can see how it needs to get released, and you can help her do it.

JM: Absolutely. No question. But, if she's involved in the process, she transforms too. The aborted soul transforms by letting go and moving on to wherever it's going. And she transforms into a different relationship with the world around her. And that's my goal. That's the ultimate thing that I can try to do. Where she takes that is up to her.

RG: You have her identify the sex of the aborted soul, and name it. And then she will start to try to have a dialog with the soul.

JM: Right.

RG: And how do you do that with her?

JM: I give her a prayer that calls the souls to her, so she can "see" the aborted soul, and it asks for love and forgiveness, and that usually elicits something from the soul—something goes back and forth.

RG: You mean the prayer offers love and asks for forgiveness? Is that correct? I know you don't like definitions, John, but here we're going to do this again. What are these things that you're offering and asking for? We say "love" and we say "forgiveness," and we think we all know what love is, but…

JM: The purpose for using the love and forgiveness, which everybody can understand—everybody knows about love. Everybody knows about forgiveness.

125

RG: I don't agree with that part. Because, I know, and I'll be honest here…

JM: They think they do…

RG: …I'll be honest here about myself. I have experienced this process with you, and I think I know a little bit about both of these two things—"love" and "forgiveness." But what I thought I knew, and what I learned about were completely different things. Using the words means nothing. Even using the words in normal everyday conversation, in relation to this process you're talking about—it means very little. And I don't think most people do know what it means, that's why I'm discussing it with you. I don't think they understand the true depth of it on a spiritual, experiential level.

JM: The whole point with Tracy was to get her to experience this. In other words, I wanted her to feel the emotion that she had with this aborted baby, and I wanted her to feel the emotion that the aborted baby had for her. I wanted those emotions to become real. So I asked her to be as loving as she can—and let's see what comes up. And a lot of times the emotional part is when you ask the baby to forgive you. That seems to be the one that gets everybody. Because it brings up the most emotion. And that's what's important.

RG: Do you have an idea what's going on there? I mean, is it because the person is becoming humble at that point?

JM: We talked about relationships before, and I said that in every relationship there's energy between the two parties. And, in this relationship between Tracy and the aborted baby what I want to do is to release the energy that is built up in Tracy—between these two. And to do that they have to exchange emotion, feel emotion, feel energy. And when they can they reach an agreement, the energies are discontinued, or disconnected—separated. And the aborted soul will move on and Tracy is left with a warm loving feeling, and that emotional constellation we talked about before, the psychological complex, is released.

RG: The actuality of forgiveness seems to be central to this.

JM: I agree. Absolutely. Love and forgiveness—very, very powerful. And in all religious thought, of course, it's central.

RG: Well, I'd like to try to address this concept of this deep love a little bit more. Now your idea is that healing comes from connecting to the universe with love. We discussed connecting. I mean, basically you're teaching Tracy how to connect. First with you, then with her emotions, and her memories and experiences, and then with the actual energy that was the connected life energy from the abortion. And she learns to connect with that. And in having all these connecting experiences, she is really learning to connect to the universe with love. That's enormous growth for her. And you have to think about her children who are going to benefit from this experience—and her husband, and everybody else that comes into contact with her. I remember when you told me this story—and just so people understand our process in writing this book—you've told me the story, and you've actually gone back into the healing experiences, and tried to transmit those to me. In this case the story of the incident that happens to her in her vision of the airplane— I'm calling that a vision, and not a dream, on purpose—this was so strong that I felt like I was standing in warm water up to my chest, and rocking in the water. That's what it felt like to me. That's this deep love that I'm talking about. People would call it love, but whether most people have had that kind of a deep experience—I know most people have an experience of love, but there is something more here that I'm trying to get at—that a person would learn by going through this process.

JM: I think that when you connect to another person, one on one, for love, it's one thing—a powerful thing—but it's one thing. When you connect to something greater than you—call it God, call it an angel, call it the Tao—I call it the universe. When you connect to that, that power is so much greater than you, and the reservoir, the amount of it, the feeling of that love is huge. It's overwhelming—much different than you'll get with one person. And that's the powerful part of it. That's the thing that you were just talking about. It's more than just love. And that's why religion is around. It's a way—it's a pathway to get to that energy. That's what people are all trying to do. And I don't mean to blaspheme, or insult anybody, but that to me is the essence of the whole thing. They all have different paths to get there, but essentially it's the same "there" they are getting to.

RG: And somehow—especially, as we've been talking about this case with Tracy—somehow the ability to ask for and receive forgiveness seems to be a key that opens the door to the deep love.

JM: I agree with that. I think it has to do with letting go of your own ego, letting go of your own sense of self-importance, and letting go of feeling like you're in control—and connecting to the other source of power and letting it flow through you. And somehow forgiveness helps open you up to that, because it makes you humble. It makes you let go of your crafty little mind that wants to control everything. And when you can, it becomes really powerful. And that's what I'm able to do with people here—is to somehow connect them to that. Usually, in the beginning, through me. And then through themselves.

RG: When you say through you, you mean you're...

JM: In other words, that's where my energy, that's where my power, that's where my strength comes from—is being able to connect with that source. And in me they can feel it, and so they're able to find their way to that source too.

Chapter 5

Gathering Your Own Power

Rose

I always felt bad. I don't mean ill. I mean bad. I felt like nothing was ever going to be alright. Ever. I always felt that I needed to apologize for just being there. You know, I was bad. Bad. Then I felt sick sometimes, but I got better. And then it got worse, and worse, until I was sick all the time. I had to have operations. On my throat for the thyroid. On my belly for endometriosis. I developed vision problems. I had irritable bowel, running to the loo all the time. I was really a mess. It got to the point where I couldn't work. I didn't want to go out anyway. By then my husband and I didn't get along. I was twenty-eight at the time I'm telling you about.

I was in absolute misery. Then the headaches started. Finally, all I wanted to do was chuck it in right then. I still don't know why I didn't. One time I had to go out to the store, and to my great embarrassment I ran into an old girl friend. I could see the shock on her face. She even started to tear up. About two weeks later she called me and gave me John Myerson's name. She insisted that I go see him right away. I wrote it down and put the paper in a drawer and forgot about it.

Several weeks later I was making coffee. The phone rang. My head just hurt from the noise, really bad. I snapped, and threw the phone across the kitchen. Then threw most of the other things in that room. I made a real mess. After that I just sank down on the floor with my back against the cabinets and sobbed, it seemed like for hours.

Next morning while cleaning up the kitchen I remembered the note. I took it out and sat down and looked at it for a while. John Myerson it said. I called and got an answering machine and left my name and number and put the note away again.

Later that day John called back. He had a nice voice, calming. I just said my friend told me to call. He said he could feel that I was in a lot of pain, and why didn't I come for an appointment. I said what did I have to lose and why not. So I made the appointment for the next week.

131

I went to John's office in Framingham. The sign said wait here so I did. John called down from the top of the stairs to come up. It was a nice, comfortable older building, and I went up the stairs and down the hall and John beckoned me into his office with a big smile. He was a large man. I sat down on the couch across from him. It was like he was just waiting for me. There was something really different about it all. And him. I don't know, maybe like the world outside was far away. It was quiet. Sounds were muffled. He had all sorts of decorations all around. I was terrified, but didn't let on. It seemed like he knew anyway.

He asked what he could do for me. At that moment I just broke down and cried. For a long time. John just sat there. He didn't come over to me. He didn't say anything. I looked up and his eyes were closed. He was smiling. It was then that I thought maybe I might some day be OK after all. Was that really possible? My throat closed up on me again thinking about that and I cried some more.

John asked me what was wrong. I told him all my symptoms and pains. We talked for a long time it seemed. Then he asked would I let him give me acupuncture. I agreed and he took me into his treatment room. It was also furnished with plants and interesting things all around. He asked me to lie down and he gave me the acupuncture treatment. He put on some quiet music and left the room, saying he would be back. I never had acupuncture before, so I didn't know what to expect. After awhile I just fell into a deep sleep, and I woke up as he was coming through the door. He removed the needles, and said to sit up slowly, and take my time. Then we went back to his office and he asked me when I wanted to come back. I made an appointment for the same time the next week and went back down the stairs and out to my car.

I don't know why I decided to go back. Maybe just telling someone my symptoms was enough of a reason. The rest of the day I noticed I felt a little different. Maybe not better, but definitely different. Was it the acupuncture? Maybe. I slept a little better too, that night. And so I felt I had made the right decision to see John again the next week. Anyway, at least I was taking some action.

I kept going to see John for several weeks. Each time we'd talk for about a half-hour and then I'd get my acupuncture treatment. Usually I'd tell him what was going on with me that week. How I felt. What I did. Was I sleeping better. Was I going out at all.

That sort of thing. No big deal, right? And I was starting to actually feel better. The headaches really were less frequent. I was thinking there might be light at the end of the tunnel.

Then one time John started to tell me things. He said I was sick because

I was all turned in on myself. He said I was hiding. At first I was startled, then shocked that he would say such things to me. He wouldn't stop, and I finally got pissed at him and started to yell, but he just calmly took it all in. Then he said it again. Now I had to take him seriously, so I asked what the hell he meant. Wasn't I there as his patient? How could he turn on me like that?

John began patiently explaining it to me again. He said if I wanted to get well I had to learn how to be myself. He said that I always gave in to other people's ideas of who I should be, and that was what was making me sick all the time. It felt like he had dowsed me with a cold bucket of water. Didn't I have medical problems? Here I thought I was doing what I was supposed to do. I went there for the appointments. I talked about myself, not an easy thing for me. And I submitted to those acupuncture treatments. Wasn't I getting better? Wasn't I improving at all?

John said yes, I was improving. But there were limits to what I could expect as a passive patient. He said I had to start changing inside. He said he wanted me to take responsibility for myself. I said how could I? He said it was something I could learn to do, and he would help me. The whole idea was just so funny. Me? I started laughing, and so did he. I laughed and laughed. Then it turned to tears. When I looked up he was still smiling. I looked away real quick, but I was feeling warm inside from it.

Each time I would see John he would make me see a little more of how things really were about me. Eventually I stopped being insulted by it. I finally figured out that he wasn't challenging me, just trying to teach me. Nobody had ever really taken the time to do that before.

He told me that I was really already alright. That it was alright to be who I already was. I thought it was ridiculous. Couldn't he see how I was in pain. Who'd want that to be who they really were anyway. He came back with the idea that it was important for me to accept myself even including the pain. He said the pain would get less from just that. I couldn't figure out what he wanted at all. Accept what?

Then he gave me a book to read, "Goddesses in Everywoman" by Jean Shinoda Bolen. He asked me to read the book and then we'd talk about it. He explained that the book used the Greek goddesses to describe different kinds of women, and he thought I might recognize myself in one or more of them. I went home and lay down on the couch and started reading. It was fascinating. This Jungian psychiatrist explained that the goddesses were patterns buried deep inside us, and whether we liked it or not, we would play out the patterns of the goddesses that were the strongest in each of us. I read about Artemis, Athena, Hestia, Hera, Demeter, and Persphone. It was interesting but no bells were ringing for me really.

Then I started reading about Aphrodite, the goddess of love and beauty. And as I read, I started remembering things that had happened when I was younger, before I started getting sick. I used to look really good, and lots of people liked me when I was a kid. I used to be the one who "kissed the boys and made them cry" in grammar school. All the boys wanted to be with me, so I could pick and choose whoever I wanted, whenever I wanted. The girls always passed the boys notes that said,

> 2 young
> +2 fall
> 4 Rose

When I was that young it seemed I was always the center of attention. Even for my beautiful handwriting. The teachers all loved me too. I had a lot of energy and was always doing something with friends. I liked to make things too, especially in art class.

Then I started to have crushes on boys in school. A lot of different boys. Now that I was thinking about it I could even remember some of the boys I liked the best. At first my parents were happy about it, saying how cute, but things changed when I started to grow up more. My mother still liked it when the boys took me out, but Daddy started getting angry at me, and scaring my boyfriends. It got so tense. We couldn't talk anymore, and he often would leave the room when I came in. I hadn't thought about these things in years. Now, remembering, I felt myself flushing, and then I felt sick and had to run to the loo.

I went to my next appointment with John, and he asked me what I thought of the book. I said I thought I was like Aphrodite. He said yes, he agreed with me about that. Did I know that there were other women like me, like Aphrodite, he wanted to know. I told him I never knew there were different kinds before. He asked did I see that what I thought was bad about me was just the way I was. I asked what did he mean. He said that I was a very sexy woman, and that was part of Aphrodite. It was just that way.

It was like a light bulb lit up in my head. I suddenly could see why people would treat me like that, like I was dirt. He asked whether I really thought I was dirt, and I said I did most of the time. He said Rose do you think that is your own idea, or other people's ideas that you believe? The light bulb went on again. I said I guessed it was other people's. He said now that you know we can do something about it. I felt dizzy for a few days after that session. I watched other people react to me and I could see it plain as day. They would shy away from me, and I would just feel bad. Really bad.

John said I was going along with them by habit, and I needed to learn how to not get taken in by other people's judgements about me. He said I had to accept my power. I asked him what power, and he said remember Aphrodite and the other goddesses. Each one has a different kind of power. For Aphrodite the power is sexual attraction. He said the next time I went out I should see if there were men watching me. I said a wreck like me. He said you'll see.

I did what he asked, and sure enough there were men and boys of all ages trying to get a look at me without being seen. Then, sometimes one would smile at me. I was truly shocked. I thought I was beyond being attractive. When I went back to John and told him he said now you know. You have the power to attract them. You always have. And now you also know what your father was afraid of, why he didn't like your boyfriends. And why he stopped liking you. I could see what he meant now.

Your father was jealous and scared, John said to me. He didn't like feeling what he felt around you, and he kept putting you down until you started believing him. It was him, not you, that felt bad. He put it on you and you still mostly believe him. That is something that we just can't have anymore, Rose. He said I think it's time that we do a separation with your father. I said what's that. John said I needed to let go of him.

I was supposed to say a prayer that John called The 27 and sit and think about my father every day until he no longer answered me in my head. John said he was also doing the separation, but that I had to do it myself. The prayer asked me to send forgiveness to Daddy for all the things he did that hurt me. To tell you the truth the last thing I felt like right then was forgiving him. I was pretty angry about it now that I saw what had happened. I told John and he said just keep at it. It will take some time but not a lot. It took me about five weeks until I could really feel the forgiveness. Then I started remembering how much fun I used to have with him when I was really young. After that the prayer really started to mean something to me.

I went to see John and he asked how the separation was going. I said I was loving my father again after all those years. All of a sudden I felt a buzzing sensation. I could feel it in the air and it made my body vibrate. It got stronger and stronger. I appealed to John. He said go with it, close my eyes and breathe, so I did. The vibrations got stronger and more powerful. I was in a totally dark tunnel. It was the darkest place I ever have been. I felt the vibrations all around me. The tunnel was very constricting and I was suffocating, but somehow I also was safe. Amazingly, I could feel John there with me, so I just kept on breathing.

Then suddenly I was out. It seemed like I was now in outer space. Then I got a shock of recognition. As I looked to my right I saw John dressed completely in black. He was wielding a long straight sword. Fire was blasting out of the sword. Five absolutely black chariots with black horses and drivers dressed in black were arrayed before me. John was directing them to remove a black shroud that covered my father and me. The shroud was draped over his head and I was underneath it. A battle raged for a long time. Then, suddenly, the sword-fire encompassed the shroud. The shroud was pulled away from me with a whooshing sound, and was rapidly carried off by the chariots to a distant area of impenetrable darkness to my left. I watched as it was slowly absorbed into the darkness. Then everything became light.

I felt light and free. I looked over to John and he was sheathing the sword he carried on his back. He smiled at me. Then I was in John's office again, with the John I knew and loved smiling the same smile at me. My body tingled. I felt terrific.

John explained what had happened. He said my father had attracted dark energy when I was young. It happened because of his anger, and then he kept feeding the dark energy everytime he got angry at me. Eventually the dark energy took over our relationship. John said that with energy that dark, you had to have a completely different kind of power to change the situation. This is what had just happened. He said my father was no longer hanging around me and the separation was over.

I felt different. I wasn't sure how, but it was definitely different. Maybe freer. Maybe less stressed. Maybe lighter. And I did notice that some of my pain had just faded away. I suddenly remembered that was the reason I went to John in the first place. I certainly never thought that my illnesses were due to anything like what John called blocked Aphrodite energy. But if it wasn't, then why did I feel so much better now?

The better I felt, the more my husband got on my case. Now I could see the difference. I'd go see John and come out feeling like there was hope and I'd go home where my husband just couldn't seem to see any difference. I told John and he said maybe your husband will learn how to change with you. Give it some time. But time passed and I learned more and more how to take care of myself and stand up for myself, but Manny just kept putting me down. John referred us to a couples counselor and to my surprise Manny said he'd go. We went every week for a month but it went nowhere. Then two months and Manny said forget it he wasn't going any more.

I discussed it with John. John asked me had I made an honest effort to keep my marriage with Manny. Was there anything more I could do. I said I didn't think so. Then he said you have a choice to make. Either you can put up with Manny the way he is, or you can leave. John was right. I just couldn't go back to being dumped on all the time. Luckily we didn't have kids, so there were no problems there. I went home and later that week

I told Manny, who surprised me by agreeing right away. I moved out that week.

I never would have believed that my problems were related to what John calls archetypal energy, or anything about feeling the love of the universe, or forgiveness, or anything else like that. But now I feel that this is true. It's really amazing how much better I feel. I'm looking forward to things again. And I keep getting better every day.

A Conversation with John Myerson on Gathering Your Own Power

This interview was conducted by Robert Greenebaum with shamanic healer John Myerson.

RG: John, let's talk about power today, and basically the whole idea of what it is, what it means to own your power, and the kinds of feelings that people have related to it—mostly fear.

JM: I would agree with the fear part. The first thing I want to say about it is that "power" does not mean "power over somebody." That's not what we're talking about. We're not talking about influencing somebody else, ruling somebody else, or doing negative things to somebody else. We are talking about an energy that we all have that's unique to us—each one of us—that gives us strength. It allows us to do certain things that other people may or may not be able to do. For example, somebody who is a child prodigy at the piano, that person's power is hearing and feeling the universe, and expressing it through the piano music—through the energy they create through their hands. That's what I call owning their power. Or the basketball player Larry Bird. He could tell you where the ball was going to be way before the ball actually got there. He could feel the pattern and flow of the game to that extent when he was "on." That was his power, his gift. That's an energy that comes through him that he uses. I would absolutely agree with you that the fear factor comes in. Most people are afraid of their own power, and part of the process that I use is to get them to a place where they can accept who they are, what their power is, and how they can use it.

RG: The examples you used are very extreme for illustration purposes. There are many, many more powers that are subtler and one person could have several. People's powers, gifts, or abilities are related to their energetic makeup.

JM: We all have some power, whatever that may be. In the realm that we are talking about there are various kinds of psychic powers—otherworldly powers. From feelings and intuitions to people who are precognitive, in other words they see the future. Some people have dreams that come true. Other people see auras. Medical intuitives can touch you or scan your body with their minds or their hands, and feel what's going on inside your body medically. Some can do this without touching you at all. There are all different kinds of powers. I think within the psychic realm there is a different flow of light and dark energies. I am not discussing evil energy, like Hitler—energy that has no good to it at all—no redeeming quality whatsoever. But in an ordinary person you have yin and yang, dark and light. Everybody has the loving side and everybody has a darker side. Each person has different powers, and each power might come through a person in a different way.

RG: Would you agree that in our society most people probably have their power withheld at some point in their childhood, or schooling? As an example, someone who is successful in business could fully accept their power in their career, but they may be in some way unhealthfully stultified in their acceptance of their own emotional power.

JM: I would agree with that, and I think it's the nature of society to do that. All societies somehow will do that to you. It's up to the person to elevate themselves, or overcome that—to whatever extent is possible for them.

RG: If you own your own power, what do you get? Why put all the effort into it?

JM: You're happy. It feels good. The most obvious thing to me is that you become comfortable in yourself. And you are not ruled by your fear. Most people are ruled by their fear.

I'll tell you a story about when I was out in California in the early seventies. It was the first time I was out there. I was in college, and we went out for Christmas break, and I stayed with some friends from my dorm. One of them took me to see a famous Indian guru who never talked. I was wondering how we're going to go hear him talk if he doesn't talk! We arrived, and the people were dressed in white robes, and a man was talking, and the guru was just sitting there. He had a certain energy to him, no question about it. And it was time for the guru to talk, and I was saying to myself, "This is going to be interesting!" He got up and went over to a black board, and wrote two words: "FEAR/LOVE," and sat down again. That was it! He didn't do another thing. And I said to myself, "What a waste of time this is. This is the biggest waste of time I've ever seen in my life." And years later it came to me what he was talking about—or not talking about—very powerfully, obviously, because I still remember this, the seed he had planted in me. You have a choice. You can live your life in fear. Or you can live your life in love. And when you own these powers, and you're OK with them, and you're OK with who you are, you can live a life in love instead of letting your fear rule you.

It's akin to a satori or an enlightenment experience in Zen, but to me it's more than that because it's on all realms. It's on the physical realm. It's on the psychological realm. And it's on the spiritual realm, too. It's a whole spectrum of feeling good about yourself. You know you can frequently see people who have had an enlightenment experience. They may be very advanced on a spiritual level, but on the psychological or interpersonal level can't function at all. I'm talking about something that encompasses all the different levels combined. So that's why you do it. When you can let go of your fears it's a very powerful thing.

RG: Owning your power is the same thing as letting go of your fears?

JM: It's part of it.

RG: Letting go of your fears is part of owning your own power?

141

JM: Correct.

RG: We've talked about connecting to the universe with love. Is owning your power achieving that, or is that a separate thing that you have to do?

JM: Again, I would say that it's part of it.

RG: Could you explain that?

JM: It's not one thing that's going to get you to own your power. It's a constellation of things. And I would say that letting go of your fear is one aspect. And connecting to the universe with love is another one.

RG: So owning your own power is a process that takes time. It's not an event.

JM: Yes. A long time for most people. And you'll have lots of events along the way. There will be many peak experiences, or satoris. It's like something "clicks" in you, and all of a sudden you get it, and the world sort of shifts. The "Aha!"

RG: That kind of experience would be what we've been calling a "healing experience."

JM: Correct.

RG: Owning your own power could be considered a part of healing, or is healing a part of owning your own power, or both?

JM: I don't distinguish it. To me it's all the same thing. I just go and see where it takes me (laughs).

RG: I know. (laughs) Here's where I'm going with this. We talk about healing. That implies you are healing from something—into something. It's a transition. And we talked a minute ago about societal stultification of people's personal power. So in some respects what we're talking about here is that healing can be owning your own power—taking back what was withheld from you earlier in your life that you were given at birth.

JM: I'm not sure I agree with that. I agree with part of it. But people come in with different karma, and so I'm not sure people come in with all their power. Because they have to overcome stuff that happened to them in the past. I see that over and over again. With that qualification I would agree with you. I don't think you have it at birth. You may have more of it at birth than you do at age twelve, or fifteen, or right now. I think that people come in with a certain already-clouded power. I've very rarely seen a little kid who was perfectly "right there." I've seen this with my own kids when they were born. Each one came in with different stuff. So, to me that's a karmic kind of thing that you come in with—which is again societal anyway, because they lived in a society before. I'm just saying that you come in with a lot of stuff also.

RG: What I meant is along the lines of Thomas Jefferson's idea that you have the right to your power. And then there are mental habits that are instilled in you along the way that keep you from it. So part of the healing process is to deal with dissolving some of those mental habits.

JM: Without a doubt. No question. That's a basic foundation of Buddhism. You have to let go of all your delusions, all those things that you trap your mind with—or are trapped in your mind.

RG: But these delusions came from somewhere. What you're saying is that you may have brought some of those delusions with you into this incarnation. Other ones you've received from people along the way and internalized. And still other ones are in the matrix of society that you just pick up by virtue of being a member of that society. It can be a complex process to deal with these. It can be time-consuming. On the other hand, some people have an imperative to do this. They cannot go on the way they're going.

JM: And those are the kind of people I deal with a lot. I'm the same way, I've always been driven to do this. I couldn't explain to you why. It's just in me. That's just what I've always done. I take that as a karmic thing. Somehow, right from the start I was programmed to do that. It wasn't in my background. My parents weren't into it. I grew up in a suburban background, and they certainly didn't encourage it. So I think it's something else in people. And also, people get to an existential crisis point in their lives where, just as you said, they've had enough of whatever it is they were doing and they want to change. Whatever it was that they were doing isn't working anymore, and they start questioning it, looking at it, and changing it. I get a lot of those kind of people here. Sometimes it's an actual physical disease that brings them to that point. Other times it's an emotional disease. And other times it's just a crisis.

RG: You mean an event, like a death in the family or a divorce?

JM: Or plain "not happy." They're walking around and they have plenty of money, a loving spouse, kids, and cars, and they're just not happy. And they have to ask themselves why they aren't they happy.

RG: How does somebody find out what their power is?

JM: Trial and error. Playing with it. Experiencing it. Going through these things that I talked about. It starts happening to you. For instance, some people start having dreams, and in the dreams they see things that come true. Other people start feeling emotions from people. They will talk to you, and on their own body they'll feel your emotions. Other people feel your thoughts. Other people might start just being happy, and the happiness leads them to do something. Or they decide they want to take up dance, and they start dancing, and dance becomes a vehicle for them. Or painting. Or singing. Other people, like me, see souls of dead people (laughs). For me, I would say, that martial arts and meditation were the vehicle initially.

RG: To accept your own power.

JM: To start accepting my own power. But it's an unfolding process. I find that I work on this all the time.

RG: In other words there is not a goal. There's not a certificate. There's no choir singing.

JM: There's no endgame. There's no "Ode to Joy". (laughs).

RG: What we're talking about is more a way of life.

JM: Correct. And it keeps on growing, and growing, and growing. And as you let go of more of your fear and you connect to the love of the universe, the happier you get, and the more of the power you feel within you.

RG: There's been a lot of discussion recently, particularly in industry and business, about "empowerment." Sometimes in other venues as well. Empowerment of workers, for instance, to determine their own job procedures, and so forth. Is that the same type of thing we're talking about here?

JM: It could be. Any kind of finding one's own way can be construed as getting your own power. But I think I'm trying to talk on a different plane here. What we're talking about now is connecting emotionally, psychically, spiritually to something that helps you with your own power. You know, when you read some of the religious works of the East and the West, it's very akin to the idea of God. Very akin to the idea of—I'm calling it the universe. Others will call it God, but there's a power that's very light. It's loving. It's warm. It's friendly. It makes you feel good. It's strong. It's amazingly overwhelming when you can connect with it. You get a joyous, joyful feeling. To me that's the reason you do it.

RG: It sounds like what you're saying is that if you can connect to your own power, then that in some way connects you to the power of the universe.

JM: The power of the universe flows through each of us. And the more you can get your mind, your fear, and other harmful emotions out of the way, the better position you are in to feel that. In other words, we're keeping ourselves from feeling it. It's there. It's always there, but we haven't "plugged in" yet. And the more you plug in, the more you feel. And the closer you feel to it, the stronger you get. And the more you start radiating and feeling the love that's out there in the universe.

RG: An individual could have an emotional block about feeling this, related to their upbringing, for instance. Or their past life experiences. While another person could have a physical block towards feeling this. You can either come at this process from the outside in, or the from the inside out, or both.

JM: To me it just matters who is in front of me—how I approach it. Some people can only deal with the physical first, so that's what we deal with. Other people can only deal with the emotional first, so that's what we deal with. It all depends on who they are, and where they're coming from, and what they want. You know, as a shaman you have to be fluid, and agile on your feet to determine who and what is in front of you. So many practitioners I see have a way of doing things, and they try to fit everybody into that way. While that way may be excellent, it doesn't work for everybody. It doesn't approach them where they are. So, that's what I try to do.

RG: And just as someone could have those types of differences, I'd like to get into the area of the archetypal energy. From my understanding, the archetypal energy is an intermediary—let's say "flavored"—energy between what you would consider to be ordinary personal energy and the universal energy. So somebody could have, for instance in the case of Rose, this Aphrodite energy, while another person could have another kind of energy.

JM: I absolutely agree with you. That was a very good explanation of what it is. In the Tao they say that there is the universe, there's the one. And the one has two—yin and yang. And yin and yang goes into the ten thousand things. So the energy flows. And as it flows it changes, and it gets influenced. The archetypes, if you're familiar with Joseph Campbell, who did a lot of work on primitive societies and the energies that you find in myths. Basically, he was famous for the study of myths. And he found that throughout all cultures in the world, no matter where they came from, or how different they were, the myths were all pretty much the same. And Jung called that an archetype. It's what he called an expression of the collective unconscious. In other words, the unconscious energy of all of us sits in a certain place in the world, and we tap into that. An archetype is an energy of that. So in Rose's case it's the archetype of Aphrodite, the goddess. And Jung tied into that also, and he gave it a psychological bent. He used the Greek gods as the archetypes you find in different people. Jean Bolen's books are excellent in that: "Goddesses in Everywoman," and "Gods in Everyman." In the story, Rose has other things, but eighty to ninety percent of her is Aphrodite. With that comes certain energy and certain problems which she had. Other people would have different problems with different archetypes. That's what archetypal energy is all about.

RG: A person could have a primary archetype, or they could have several that are more or less equal, depending upon who they are.

JM: Any combination.

146

RG: What would an example of just one or two of the others?

JM: There are lots of Greek ones. You name any of the gods, Zeus, or Apollo, or Athena, or Diana, or Persephone. There are other ones that other people have outlined, like the warrior, lover, king, healer. They don't have to have the Greek names. You can look at it different ways.

RG: Some other cultures have used animals for this.

JM: Absolutely.

RG: That type of energy could also be considered archetypal. Somebody could be "a turtle", for instance.

JM: Yes, the Native Americans are heavily into that—the archetypal energy of the animals. To me it's all the same thing, just a different way of talking about it.

RG: Somebody might be more related to summer, while another person might be more related to winter—in feelings.

JM: You can have any system you want. There are lots of them out there.

RG: What I'm trying to say is that these are actual natural forces in the world that the person is naturally aligned with, in one way or another. They're not just abstract intellectual systems.

JM: Yes, the Tarot is another system. The forces that are talked about—the Major Arcana—are just that. They are major archetypal energies.

RG: In that case you might have "a hermit" that would indicate someone who felt more comfortable by him- or herself, for instance.

JM: Right.

RG: To go back to the whole concept of owning your own power, it's not necessarily that you have to know and study archetypes, but I think our point here is that there is natural energy in the world that an individual taps into naturally by virtue of who he or she is.

JM: And my point in owning your own power is that you have to *be* that. You have to experience it and be OK with it—OWN IT!—you have to be it. It has to fit you. You have to be OK with being that. For example, someone might want to have the "healer" archetype, but his energy is a "king" archetype. It may not be what you want it to be. That happens all the time—what we're good at. You know, somebody can sprint, but they want to run a marathon. I notice this in my daughter. She has beautiful curly hair. All she wants is straight hair. So you have to be OK with what you have, what's actually there, not what you want it to be. That's where the problem comes in. Everybody wants a certain thing, but you have to be OK with what you actually are, and have, in this lifetime.

RG: At some point that means giving up your attachment, or your desire, to be another way. It also means taking responsibility for who you are, and the way you are.

JM: And using it. Expressing it. Acting like it. And being alright with whatever it is that you are. Some of it comes with age. My desire to be like Greg LeMond on the Tour de France, cycling over the Pyrenees—you know I'm too old for that now. (laughs) I had to give that one up. I'll never be like Muhammed Ali.

RG: That brings up an interesting point, though, because people at different ages, and different parts of their lives could be more related to different archetypal energies than at another stage.

JM: It's true. Another thing to accept is where you are in your life. What is that energy you have in your life, and what can you do to express it.

RG: There's a certain concept of reflection involved in this. In other words, reflecting on who you are, that's very traditionally religious. For instance, one of the main functions of a monastery is to provide a space for reflection. However, you don't have to be "over the hill" in order to own your own power. As a matter of fact, it would be nicer if you could do it before then.

JM: Yeah, I think it would be great. I think the sooner you start the better you're going to be. And it doesn't have to be organized religion. I would absolutely agree that it is spiritual. I would absolutely agree that it has to do with connecting to the universe, or to God, or to The

One, or to the Spirit, or whatever you want to call it. You definitely can get there, and it can help you using organized religion. But you do not have to have, or be part of an organized religion to do this. And the thing that I like about the shamanic practices is that anybody can do it. It applies to any organization, any religion, any type, any person, any culture in the world at any time. And because of that it doesn't have any of the problems that can be endemic to organized religion—the structure, the politics, the expression, and the fact that wherever you go in the world someone is not going to like someone else because they are different. The energy that I'm talking about with shamanic practice is at the basis of all the religions and all spiritual work. Being the old Zen man here, I don't like the forms. You can do it. You don't need to have someone else do it for you.

RG: What do you mean by that?

JM: You have to do it yourself. You have to take responsibility to do it yourself. The priest, or the rabbi, or the guru is not going to do it for you. You have to do it. And I'm not putting them down. I'm just making a statement that wherever you are, in whatever system you choose, you still have to do it.

RG: "You have to walk that lonesome valley by yourself," from the old song, right.

JM: I love it.

RG: In my personal experience, I first came across this idea in real life—not in a book—during a Native American powwow. Before the drumming and dancing started, a woman got up. I do not know whether she was a tribal leader. She definitely was not an elder. I'd say she was in her mid-twenties. And she said, "As all of us are doing, I am trying to own my own power." It just completely spun my head around. At the time I had never thought of it like that at all. I probably was in my late thirties then, and still fairly unconscious about most things. So that's how I first came across this concept. In my personal experience it can be an intense process, but it doesn't have to be intense. It depends upon the time of your life, what you're going through, who you are, what you want—because certainly your desires about who you want to become are definitely involved in this.

JM: And the nature of what it is that you have to go through. If you are working on fear, it's going to be more intense than working on something else, depending upon what fear it is, and how you're working on it.

RG: To be specific, we're not talking about, for instance, developing new professional skills here. You could, for example, if you realized your desire was to address people on a specific subject of your choice, and that was owning your own power, you could go take speech lessons.

JM: Anything that causes fear that you have to go through could be used.

RG: It's your obstacle.

JM: I agree with that. But it's greater than that. That's in this realm here. You have to take it to the other realms also. So you have to take it to the psychological, emotional, and spiritual realms also. On the physical plane I agree with you, physical things can be used. But you need to take it to another place also.

RG: Or recognize the other changes that are going on in you as a result of doing something, for instance, career-wise. This could be viewed as one long series of tunnel experiences.

JM: You could look at your life as an entire tunnel, too, if you wanted to. You keep on travelling through with little stops along the way. And I think that the topic that I talked about before, about the light and the dark parts of ourselves—the "shadow" parts of ourselves, needs to be looked at even more. Because there's a feeling, especially in the New Age stuff that I see, that anything that's of "the shadow," or of "the dark" is not "good." You want to get rid of it. So everybody walks around with smiles, and everything is "fine." But, see, to me the important thing is to be real. And anger is real, fear is real, pain is real. Love is also real. But these other emotions are part of us. We're human! And to deny that we have them is not real either. So you're never going to be "without fear." You're never going to "not have any anger." You're never going to "not feel anybody else's, or your own, pain." You need those things. They help you through life. If you can't connect to your pain, you can't connect to someone else's pain, you can't help them heal. You can't deny them. You just have to be OK with them. It's like your mind is a boardroom table. And around the table are all kinds of things: fear, anger, jealousy, all kinds of sub-personalities, personas, masks that we wear. But there's only one chairman, and you're the chairman. But what happens a lot of times is that fear becomes the chairman. Fear runs that boardroom. No, that's not the way it is. Fear is only one member of the board. And so you have to be OK with all those members around the table, whether they're ones you want to be OK with, or not. When fear comes up, you don't necessarily want that. On the other hand, it's a message: "Be careful! Look out! Something's going on! Pay attention!" You can make fear your ally. You can use the energy that fear gives you. It's an energy. You can use that. You can become an ally to that. But you don't want to let it run you, because then you are living in fear. Anger is that way also. Anger gives you a lot of power, but you don't want to let that power run you. You want to use it as a tool that you have control over, that you're OK with, wherever you are in that spectrum.

RG: To go in a different direction, one of the things that often holds people back from owning their own power is a feeling of being ashamed of who they are because of whatever their life experiences have been. Particularly, in relation to the story of Rose, now we're talking about a love energy, but it's also a sexual energy. In her case, she was made to feel that it wasn't OK to have this energy. It wasn't OK for her to be who she was, therefore she acquired feelings of self-shame. Talking about obstacles, this is an enormous obstacle for somebody to get through.

JM: Shame is one of the worst. There's no question. It's akin to fear because it freezes you. And it's definitely a learned kind of behavior that you get. And the problem with Aphrodite energy, as in Rose's case, is that it's such a primal sexual thing that she can't not have it. On the other hand, society doesn't want that kind of energy running around free. And so, somebody like Rose is going to have a problem with any society that she lives in, because it's always trying to control her. And what you can't control is that kind of basic energy, especially sexual energy. A big part of the process with Rose was owning her power—recognizing that she was Aphrodite. What does that mean to her? How does that get expressed? How did it get squashed? What were all the ways? Learning to walk down the street, do you feel free? Or do you feel shame? Going to the beach in your bathing suit, what do you feel? Finding places where she identifies how her father made her feel ashamed, how her husband always made her feel ashamed, and feeling those in real life, and then being able to let go of them—what I call separations—separating from those attachments to her shame: That's where you gather your power. And each one that you separate from, you "let go of," you "become OK with" you gather more power. So, it's a process. The shame is something she learned over her life. She's going to have to let go of it over the rest of her life.

RG: The shame is kind of a numbing. She can't feel her real self. What she feels is a kind of a shell that has been put on her.

JM: And if she feels anything at all, she feels bad about herself. Guilt is one thing. Guilt is if you say, "Oh, I did that wrong. I'm sorry." Shame is, "I did that wrong. Oh, I'm terrible! I'm worthless. I'm no good at all." It's a way deeper kind of feeling, that base fear of not being good enough. That's the problem with shame. Every time she would walk by a group of men, she'd feel ashamed. And she hadn't done anything wrong. She didn't do anything.

RG: Right. She just was who she was.

JM: And lots of women have a part of Aphrodite in them, like lots of men have a part of Aries, or Mars, the god of war, in them. Not all men, not all women, but a lot. The thing with Rose is that she had about eighty per cent of Aphrodite—a lot!

RG: Let's talk about your treatment style a little bit, particularly in relation to "Aphrodite women," because I know that you have had a number of patients with a similar problem, although their life situations were all quite different. One of the issues with this is that they are very female, and you are male. How do you deal with that problem?

JM: For some reason I attract a lot of Aphrodites. I guess—you know astrologically I am Aries (laughs). I'm very much Aries, and Aries was the husband of Aphrodite in Greek mythology. But I do attract a lot of Aphrodites, probably because of the power or energy that I have. However, I am able to detach myself from it. I'm able to be very present and loving to them, but let them know that it's going no further than that. We connect, but we don't touch physically. And I think that's very important for Aphrodites to understand. And every Aphrodite that I deal with, we have to go through that. They try to seduce me. And that's their nature. They put the Aphrodite energy out, and it's seducing. And I encourage them to do that, because that's Aphrodite. But I let them know that's all it is. That's what it is. That's what we're dealing with. And that's as far as it goes between them and me. And I think they appreciate that. I think they appreciate someone actually knowing what's going on inside of them, and accepting them for that, and not trying to seduce them for that. And for some reason, thankfully, my karma this time around is that it doesn't affect me. I didn't say that I'm unaware of that. I am aware, but I'm able to not succumb to it. I have been eternally thankful every time I work with them. It's very difficult to do. They are very good at manipulating men. But for some reason it just doesn't affect me. I can see that energy coming at me, and I'm able just to see it for what it is, and accept it for what it is.

RG: I'd like to talk a little bit about the process. On the one hand you have your patient, who is probably a somewhat numb person, because of the experiences that she's gone through. On the other hand she has this very strong Aphrodite/love/sexual energy that is part of her, and that she is tapped into as we've discussed previously. You can see through her shame personality to her archetypal energy. And you have to work through that. I'm curious about when you start working with somebody: how does this look to you shamanically? Can you see a route to get in somehow immediately, or does it take a long time?

JM: It depends. I've had both situations. But what I try to do with every person that comes in here is I connect heart to heart with him or her. I try to get some connection, not on this level. It's on a different realm with people. I think every good therapist tries to do that. I try to do that right away. When I do that with an Aphrodite woman, the Aphrodite vibration comes out. In other words, I feel it in a certain way from experience. I've seen lots and lots of Aphrodites, so I know that vibration very, very well. When I recognize it, then I realize that what I need to do is get her to feel it also. Now some of them are in touch with it, and some of them are totally, totally numb. If she is in touch with it, then we can talk about it and feel it. If she is not, and she is totally numb and shamed by the whole thing, then I have to go the archetype route. I back up, and I go the psychological, cognitive way. I listen to her story. I tell her I understand the story. I relate what's going on with it. I bring out the books on archetypes. I have her read about Aphrodite. I get a connection so that psychologically she understands what's going on—before we get into the vibration part.

RG: Or really, the "feelings" part.

JM: Correct. So, it depends on where she is when she comes in. Either way, it always starts with that connection. I get the vibration. So I would say, with an Aphrodite I don't necessarily see anything. I feel it. There's a vibration in the room that I feel, that I know. And some of them are so obvious it's amazing. You don't have to be psychic to figure this out. This is just who they are. But other ones, you know—it's very interesting. I had one girl who comes to mind. She was sixteen or seventeen, maybe eighteen. Very mouse-like. She doesn't say anything. And very withdrawn. And very dark. And when I looked at her psychically I got that vibration. I almost didn't believe it. She didn't exude that at all. So what I did with her was that I questioned her. I said, "Do you ever let yourself out?" I think she knew exactly what I was talking about. The first I saw it was in her eyes. I got the flash in her eyes, and as soon as I made contact with that I said to myself, "Aha!" I said to her, "Why don't you ever let that out?" She said because if she's in the classroom everybody can see her. If she's wherever, everybody notices her. If she's in the mall, people look at her. And she doesn't want any of that. So she hides it. The hiding of it is making her sick, which is why she came to me to begin with.

RG: It seems to me that there's an enormous amount of pain involved in keeping your light under a bushel like that.

JM: Oh, had to be. She was extremely ill. She had been ill for a long time. Her situation was fascinating, because an article that had been written about me in a local town newspaper on the shamanic healing was given to her mother by her doctor. I don't usually get that kind of referral! (laughs)

RG: When a new Aphrodite patient comes to see you, there is going to be an adjustment period where you build up trust with the person. At some point they are going to have their first breakthrough. Particularly in Rose's case, the breakthrough was what aspect?

JM: I'd say the first part was when she understood what Aphrodite energy is, and acknowledged it in herself intellectually and psychologically. I don't mean spiritually yet, just that the concept clicked in her head cognitively. We had talked about it. We had talked about her experiences. She read Bolen's book on goddesses. She understood what it was, and it was like an, "Aha! That's me! There's someone else out there like this! I'm not alone in the universe! Someone understands what it is I'm talking about!" When she made that connection, that was the first step, and it was a big step!

RG: And that starts breaking down that crust of shame.

JM: Absolutely. And trusting me. Because I know who she is now, and I still will talk to her. I'm not ashamed of who she is. She's not "bad." I will still talk to her. As a matter of fact, I tell her it's a good energy to have. It's positive. It's her! Anything that's her is positive.

RG: What was the next major breakthrough?

JM: I would say the next one was realizing what her husband was doing to her. Realizing how he was putting her down. How he was keeping her ashamed. How he was thwarting her energy. And her decision to get a divorce, and to separate from him—psychically, was the next major breakthrough for her. That was whenever she was ready. I didn't suggest that she get a divorce. I suggested that she work with her power. She noticed that when she went home she would have to hide it again. At home she would be what she used to be, and outside she could be something else. Then she would go home and feel terrible again. She noticed that. So I suggested that she start talking to her husband about it. She found that she couldn't talk to her husband. So I suggested couples work with a person whom I've recommended to people. She did that, and that didn't work either. But I've seen with Aphrodites that their relationship with their husbands totally changes. Some of them stay together and their relationship grows, so you never know in advance how this will work out. It all depends on the two of them. In this particular case with Rose it didn't work. So, the second part of her work was that.

RG: Coming to terms with her husband.

JM: Correct. So she could feel free at home. And the third one was when she separated from her father. Because her father was the source of most of her shame when she was young. Her husband was an external heavy force, very strong, that you could feel. Her father was sticky and gummy, and underneath. Like this dark sticky thing all over her, that was more subtle, but harder to realize. And harder to let go of.

RG: In each of these steps, in larger or smaller chunks, she is owning her own power.

JM: The first was the recognition of what her power was. And the other two were separating from males who had kept her down—who had taken away her power. Whenever you separate from someone you are owning your own power. You are taking back the power that you had given them.

RG: John, what is it that makes you want to do this difficult work?

JM: The idea and nature of power is near and dear to my heart. I think it's near and dear to every shaman's heart. It gets me excited to talk about it. I like it because to me that's the Way. That's what I do. I cultivate power. And the Aphrodite energy is just so exciting to work with. Usually when people come to me with Aphrodite energy they are so hurt, and so shamed and so full of fear. And to see them come out the other side—after a process that we go through that can be terrible—like a gorgeous flower. They've owned their power, and to me that's such a beautiful thing. It's such a great thing to watch, and be a part of its happening. And have it happen in a safe way for them, so they can relate to a man again without having all the other stuff that went on before. That this is possible for them is rewarding and exciting to me. And I love doing it.

I like the idea of power anyway. It gets me excited. It's the one thing I have the most trouble teaching to people, that excitement about power. But that's what I get the most excited about—on any realm, whether it's a sports realm, a psychological realm, or a spiritual realm.

RG: That excitement is typically squashed very early in a person. Then it's hard for people to deal with.

JM: Oh yeah. And it's hard for me, for example, as a martial arts teacher. I haven't taught that in years and years. The major reason I stopped was that I couldn't communicate that. I couldn't get that across. I couldn't get that idea and that feel—the power that people can generate and connect to. Because, you know, martial arts is very archetypal also—that warrior archetype that people connect to. It's a very primal energy that I've connected to since I was very little. I like connecting to it, not in any kind of way with aggression. But it's like Aphrodite. It's a power that these women need to connect to because it's them. But the same is true with the Aries energy, or the warrior energy. It's out there, and people need to connect to it in a way that's safe, and they can use it constructively in their lives, instead of using it with fear and power over people and causing destruction and harm.

RG: Or in another case, a person could have a lot of Aries energy, and be angry all the time, and not understand why.

JM: Absolutely. Angry all the time, and aggressive—in your face. That's what I always used the martial arts for, to get in touch with that archetype within me, which is very strong. And like a lot of people, I have different archetypes within me that are very strong. Some of them are at opposite ends of the spectrum, and getting in touch with each one has been what I do for me in my life.

RG: That's your process for owning your own power.

JM: That's my Way, capital "W."

Appendix

A Conversation with John Myerson

on

Healing & Training

This interview was conducted by Robert Greenebaum with shamanic healer John Myerson.

RG: From your point of view, what is healing?

JM: Healing takes place in an instant. Getting to that place can take a long time. So, a lot of shamanic healing is strange, because it doesn't seem like it relates to anything. But what we're really trying to do is get you to that place where you can leap, and then you heal. So, that's what I do. I try to get people to that place. Each day to take a leap. Each day to connect with me, heart to heart. Each day to feel something else besides this reality. I feel that healing takes place from the subtle to the gross. From the psychic and spiritual planes down through the emotional, mental and physical planes. And so, to effect healing you need to start—or at least somehow feel—on the more subtle planes. When people can get to the other world—nonordinary states of reality—healing takes place spontaneously, whatever the problem is. Healing in one word is change.

RG: But it has to be change in a certain direction.

JM: We have no control over that.

RG: You can change and deteriorate.

JM: Correct. And that would not be healing.

RG: What do you mean by planes? Are there actually thresholds, or is it all a continuum?

JM: It is a continuum. But like most people, I usually think of them as planes. Because it's easier to look at shelves, than it is to look at something that just flows. But it's more like pearls on a string. Each one is connected, but each one is also separate. The problem with the whole continuum is that it's not a straight line. So some people may have access to one particular part, but not to the others. And so, wherever any person is, that's where we are going to have to start. You can start anywhere on the continuum. But from my perspective, I need to start wherever that person is, not where I want them to be.

RG: And you know where they are from your own experience of going...

JM: Of touching them, and talking with them, and being with them. For example, some people are so open psychically that the goal of the treatment is to bring them back here. So they're not in touch with the physical plane at all, and I have to bring them from there to here. That's rare. What's much more common is that people are into the physical plane, and not into the other ones. And, what's even more common, is that people are into the mental plane, and are not in touch with their bodies or their spiritual psychic planes.

RG: Somebody can be ill on any of those planes.

JM: I'm not sure I'm saying on any plane. I'm just saying that you need a harmonious flow with all of them for healing to take place. Something needs to change. You said change could go backwards, and then it is not good. But, I'm not sure I agree with that. To me, change is all I'm looking for. If they didn't change they'd still go downhill. That's not change to me. When someone comes with a problem, they're heading downhill. If I do nothing, they still stay downhill and they deteriorate. That's not change to me. Change is something that makes the ball roll differently. It makes the terrain change so it's not necessarily downhill anymore. It's flat, or up.

RG: Since you said that healing takes place from the subtle to the gross, do you see, or experience, that there is a continual emanation of energy from the subtle?

JM: Yes, I would say that's true. The energy of the universe comes from the subtle.

RG: That's spiritual energy coming from someplace? It feels like it's coming out?

JM: I couldn't tell you where it comes from. It comes out and it exists outside of you, and also inside of you.

RG: People are like springs, like a water spring? The energy keeps coming from some source through people.

JM: If you're open to it, that's correct. You can always access it.

RG: Is healing helping that flow?

JM: I would agree with that. However, on a physical level your own energy that you are born with is finite. So on this plane of physical reality you are obviously not here forever. What the Taoists meant when they talked about immortality was that you could—like a Tibetan Buddhist—control the way you die, and the way you leave this body into the next plane, keeping it all together. Which means that you become immortal. They weren't stupid. They didn't think that this physical body goes on forever.

RG: What do you do to help people heal?

JM: I connect. On any plane I can, body, mind or spirit, I connect. I tell stories, or we laugh together, or we do something that's connecting on the mind level. That will lead me somewhere else. I connect. When I connect, things happen. That's my power, to make things happen. My energy is to make things vibrate, to make things happen, to make things change, charge, and feel, and do. And that's what I hope to do with people—just to make something happen. You'll find that each shaman has one or two or three techniques that they'll use. That's all, and they just go from there, as it happens. The skill is to make it happen, and to know what to do when it does happen. So, for example, with Alethea, we're sitting there, and she's telling me about the dream, and all of a sudden the dream is real. She's in the dream, I'm in the dream, and the room is vibrating big time. Did I stop and say, "Oh, look at this, isn't this nice? Would you like to go on?" No. No. No. I just go. I didn't ask, I just went. When I get to that place, I just go. I don't think, I just do. I leap. I jump as far and fast as I possibly can, dragging the person with me, and we'll see what happens. That's what I do. Sometimes it's very subtle and very gentle. And sometimes it's wrenching. So whatever happens, when someone has done this with me once, they are never the same.

I also use a lot of humor. It makes me more human, breaks the tension, and lets me in closer. I'm very tricky. Very, very devious. People think I'm a very straightforward person. And I am. In many ways I'm sort of honorable, and old-fashioned, and very, very straightforward. On the other hand, I am very, very devious. Not dishonest, but very tricky. Not calculated, just tricky. I am never just sitting here. I never do that. I am always probing, I am always moving, I am always playing. But, as soon as I see an opening, I go. If I feel even a little bit of an opening, I go. I firmly believe that when you see it, you go for it, as in Zen. There's no screwing around, you've got to really go. So while I'm laughing, and being human, and nice, I'm really moving way in. That's a trick of the trade. It's especially useful with people who keep me away. The more I can get them to laugh, the closer I am. I am very serious a lot of the time. But I find things flow better for me when it's lighter. I have a tendency to get very, very serious. So this keeps me light, and airy, and not too heavy. My energy tends to be very heavy. People can't take that, so I have to lighten up somehow. And I do that through humor.

RG: What is it that you are making happen?

JM: Change. I'm making things change. I never have any idea where it's going to go, how it's going to change. I just want to see movement.

RG: What are you trying to change?

JM: I'm trying to get people into a different place. I'm trying to get people into a non-ordinary state of consciousness. I'm trying to get people to experience something that's different. That's going to shake them up. That's going to change them. And when that happens, things change. Psychological walls fall. Emotions that never were felt before are felt. Energetic chakras open so the physical flow of energy is happening.

RG: It can be a whole range from very transcendental and joyful all the way to severely stressful.

JM: No question. And a lot of what people will feel is pain. Crying, fear— not nice things. But to me it doesn't matter. They are all the same. I want them to feel all of them.

RG: Some people say, "I never want to do that again, but I had to go through it." What do you feel about that kind of an attitude?

JM: Well, I look at emotional pain as a gift. I look at that as something that helps you open your heart chakra. In the heart chakra you get love and joy and pain. And if you can't feel that pain, then you're never going to experience the joy. The pain allows you to empathize with others' pain, and if you can do that you will be a lot happier. And you will help a lot of people. And the world would be a whole lot better place if people could feel others' pain.

RG: Who was your teacher?

JM: My teacher is a Spanish woman who grew up in Kenya. Her father fled Franco and went there. She grew up in a very rural village, where they were the only white people. At age three the village shaman adopted her. And she tells the story that her mother was very Catholic, so it was a very interesting upbringing for her. She worked with the shaman until he died. Then, when her father died, she and her mother moved back to Spain.

RG: What is your tradition?

JM: These particular people in Kenya were the Kikuyu. That's the largest group in Kenya. It's Bantu shamanism, which is ancestor worship. There is no real tradition, since we are not in Africa. I'm not African. The village ancestors are not here. It was changed by my teacher, and then changed again by me. Each person who takes it changes it. But that's where this originated. I apprenticed with her. Then she gave me permission to go on alone. A lot of the teaching is like a Dharma transmission, very personal.

RG: How long did that process actually take?

JM: Ten years.

RG: What is a shaman?

JM: Someone who is able to mediate between this world and other worlds. A shaman goes into other worlds to gain power for healing, or whatever else he or she is going to do. The theory being that—as we talked about before—the healing takes place from the subtle to the gross. If you go into the subtle realms you can find something that's amiss, and you deal with it, or right it, or help right it. That reflects back onto the gross levels.

RG: What is the interior world?

JM: I'm not sure where it is, if that's what you're asking. Supposedly, if you study modern physics, they'd say that this is one world, but there are many other worlds happening simultaneously. And so, I imagine, somehow, that's what we're tapping into. I really don't know what it is. I'm not sure how to describe it.

RG: The question I'm asking is not for a rational explanation, but what are the characteristics? What is it like? Supposedly we all know from dreams, but...

JM: I would say the major thing you feel first is that the energy level is increased. The deeper you get into it, the deeper that is. The rules in that level are not the same as here. I mean, you do things like you do in your dreams. You leap tall buildings, and you jump off whatever, and do all that kind of stuff. So it's not the same physical reality as you get here. However, there are ways to navigate it. Once I find a place in it—get the coordinates of where someone is, or where a soul is, or a place—I can find my way back very quickly.

RG: So, part of the process you use with people is finding that out, getting your bearings with them?

JM: Yes, that's correct. It's mysterious to me too. What I am doing is to open the doorway into that other place. Once you go in the door, the first thing you feel is that things vibrationally feel stronger.

RG: You feel it in your body?

JM: Yes, I feel it all over my being, but definitely in my body. You know there are different kinds of people. There are people who hear things in the other realms, there are people who see things in the other realms, and there are people who feel or sense things in the other realms. Usually people do one thing in a major way, and the other ways in lesser manner. I tend to feel or sense things, and sometimes I see them. I don't usually hear things. But sometimes I do.

RG: Is it different for you than your own dreams, or is it similar?

JM: Everything is the same to me. I'm not sure how to answer that question. The difficulty I'm having in all this is that everything is the same to me. You're asking me to describe...

RG: You could just throw me out!

JM: I don't usually dream just "dream" dreams. What I dream are journey dreams, of doing something, or being somewhere. And most often they are lucid nowadays, in that once I realize where I am, and what's going on, it's really no longer a dream. I'm moving in it, and changing it. Very rarely do I actually have just a plain dream anymore, so it's all the same to me.

You can feel it. When I go into something with energy, it changes. You can feel that on your body. For example, if someone tells me their story, the first thing I would do is I would sense their vibrations to see if they are real. Because a lot of people just make things up in their heads, and to me that is just delusion. That's not what I am after. But if the story actually feels real to me, I know it feels real because the energy vibrations from them increase whenever they talk about their stories. So then I match that. I make myself vibrate along with them. Then I can make their bodies vibrate more. And then, BINGO! I'm usually there. There is no transition. All of a sudden I am in their interior worlds, or scenes. When that happens the vibrations really increase.

RG: Then you become active at that point?

JM: No, I'm active all the way through. Because I'm the one who opened that door for them. The technique that I use is really to make the vibrations increase. And I see what happens. That's my major technique, I would say. And I just sense where to go with it. And I move very quickly when I sense it, so I don't lose it. But none of this is planned.

RG: You just deal with what comes in the door, as opposed to thinking it out ahead of time?

JM: Correct. I don't plan with each person what happens ahead of time. I do write down notes about what did happen, after each session, but I very rarely review it before the session. Very rarely.

RG: Is that the same way you handled your acupuncture practice, when it was primarily acupuncture?

JM: Pretty much so. That's just the way I'm most comfortable. Even with regular acupuncture I always took a diagnosis, but I never really followed it. I did it because that is the format you learn to get into it with someone.

RG: But acupuncture is, in fact, a shamanic tradition, in that it is dealing with primal energy.

JM: Yes. And also the early founders of the art were shamans. Absolutely.

RG: Throughout your healing career, from the beginning, you have dealt with the shamanic side, and then added layers of additional...

JM: I didn't know it at the time, however. I had no idea what I was actually doing. I knew I was using intuition, or "gut", or something like that. I didn't know it was actual, whatever it was. But you're right, I actually always used gut. I used to pick herb formulas based on that too.

RG: Intuition is the process of tapping into the archetypal consciousness. So that is also a similar technique.

JM: Yes. You know, when I go to the library to get a book, I just run my eyes along the shelves, and whichever book jumps out at me I take. I just look and see. Sometimes it's visual, which one jumps out at me. But a lot of times it isn't visual, it's just something that jumps out at me. And, as soon as I enter the library I'll know whether I'm going to find a book or not. There are days, you go in there and there's just nothing, and you just forget it.

RG: Let's talk about your career for a moment. Your first practice was acupuncture, then psychology. And sort of overlapping that was the shamanic training which you had with your teacher. So, when you were studying psychology, it's not the same as if someone were coming straight out of undergraduate school and going right into the study of psychology. You already had a decade or more of private practice behind you. And at the same time you were involved with a different kind of training, and a primordial healing method. Tell me a little about the psychology training, and how that fits in with the rest of this.

JM: Well, my dissertation was on the use of acupuncture to induce non-ordinary states. I would do the drumming work that I now use in some of my seminars, and I'd use acupuncture in addition to it. And what I found was that the acupuncture did a couple of things. The first thing is that it allows people to go into the trance state, into that other realm, easier. It lowers what I call the "sensory barrier," the barrier between a conscious and an unconscious state. And the second thing I found is that it makes the journey easier. There is a lot less tetany, cramping, yelling, screaming, whatever. It makes things much calmer and mellow, which allows you to get to a deeper process. I think it does that by increasing the energy of the situation. I experimented a lot while I was doing it, and one time I had someone put the needles in, I went into the journey, and then I had them take the needles out in the middle of the trance. Usually the needles stay in the whole way, and then we take them out. And what I found was that when someone pulled the needles out in the middle of the trance, it was like the electricity was turned off. The whole thing just crashed. My theory is that acupuncture induces a mild trance state in and of itself, and it helps power the situation. Like the drums. The drums and the bells increase the power also.

RG: The drumming is the type of drumming that is meant to induce a trance, and it is being used in addition to acupuncture?

JM: Yes, shamans have used lots of techniques to get people into trances. They've used singing, dancing, and playing musical instruments. Drums, rattles, bells being the most famous of those.

RG: And herbs.

JM: They used psychotropic herbs. Ayhuasca, mescaline, peyote. So, what I do is I use the drums. I like the drums a lot. And I use acupuncture.

RG: You also don't need the drums to do a lot of the work that you do, right?

JM: Usually I don't use the drums. Sometimes I do take people on drumming journeys here, as part of the treatment process. But a lot of the time I don't need to do that. I can just increase their vibrational energy by being here with them. In the beginning I used to use the drums, candles and other things with everybody. But as I've evolved, I realized that I've gotten stronger, and I don't need to do that. Traditionally the shaman would take the journey for the person or with you.

RG: Actually in primitive societies the person who is being treated is almost in a catatonic state.

JM: Yes. The trance for that patient is induced by the process that they are going through.

RG: I suppose the acupuncture is similar in that way. You don't move during acupuncture, though you have a lot of interior activity.

JM: Yes, and the shaman will use drummers, dancers, herbs, whatever, to increase the power and the vibration of it.

RG: You have a widely varied background in general, and in addition to your healing arts specifically, you have long been involved with internal style Chinese martial arts. There is a healing tradition that is related to the martial arts. What is that relationship, and how does that relate to your work here?

JM: Well, for me, I got into all this through Chinese martial arts. When I was fourteen or fifteen I started studying Kung Fu, and as soon as I got a little older, in high school, I used to go down to Chinatown in Boston. The sifus all had some kind of healing art. They did massage or Tui Na, which is kind of like massage and chiropractic adjustment. A couple of them did external herbs. I didn't see anybody doing any acupuncture. It was illegal at the time, but I don't think any of them were trained at acupuncture. Just acupressure massage.

I started internal martial arts when I was nineteen or twenty. That's early for internal martial arts. I was attracted to the internal arts very early, because I could also see that doing Kung Fu, or external style Chinese martial arts, for a long time you'd get hurt. First my knee went, then my back went. And I'm big, so I knew that I wasn't going to last that long. I wanted something that was going to keep me going, which is why I picked Taiji.

As far as the internal aspect, it's related to Taoist philosophy and meditation. I think there is a strong shamanic influence in Chinese medicine and Taoism. The early Taoists were nature shamans.

RG: When you started the internal martial arts had you already been meditating prior to that?

JM: I began meditating about the same time. The Taiji teacher would have us sit quietly for a little while before class. And then I got interested in meditation, and I started doing meditation from books. The first book I found was Phillip Kapleau's "Three Pillars of Zen." That had a big influence on me. And John Blofeld's book on Taoism was also a big influence on me.

My first formal meditation experience was at Phillip Kapleau's zendo in Rochester, N.Y. He was the closest Zen master. In 1971, we borrowed my father's car, four or five of my roommates, and we drove through a snowstorm to Rochester, N.Y. He had, every now and then, a day-long introductory session on Zen. And you'd sit for twenty minutes, and then walk, and then sit. Then I sat with his people in Cambridge for a while. Afterwards I became interested in Taoism, and I didn't do much more formal Zen sitting until the late seventies.

171

RG: You told me a story about a Zendo in Cambridge.

JM: I met my teacher, Maureen Stewart Roshi, in 1978 or '79, and it was before she was a Roshi. She moved into the Cambridge Buddhist Association, and then she used to have sitting in her house in Newton. I studied intensely with her until '86.

RG: You mentioned that the martial arts sifus had herbal medicine they used as external treatment for bruises and contusions. And then you got involved in meditation as well. Both those things are also related to your current work. What is the relationship?

JM: Well, I look at shamanic work as applied Zen. Zen is great. it gives you a lot of focus, but it didn't really help me to let go, or actually do anything. So, to me, shamanic healing is applied Zen. You use the focus, or the technique of Zen. You know, my therapy is very Zen-like. I'm very Zen Buddhist in my foundation. When I talk philosophically, I'm basically talking as a Buddhist, or a sort of a Taoist-Buddhist.

RG: One of the major tenets of Buddhism is releasing, or letting go, especially "worldly" issues, in their view. But that could also be applied in a therapeutic situation, I imagine, to whatever is going on.

JM: Absolutely. My actual talk therapy is very Buddhist. And that's basically the whole point of everything, to get people to a place where they can let go of it.

RG: So the meditation is part of your daily practice?

JM: Absolutely. It's also how I get to an altered state—through meditating. I'll start by sitting, and then I get into a meditative state, and then I call the souls. So, to me, literally, it is applied Zen. It's Zen doing something.

RG: So that is your "Way of Healing"?

JM: Yes. It just sort of evolved. It wasn't like this was a master plan. I started out in martial arts. Then I got attracted to meditation. I sort of bungled into each thing. I bungled into my teachers as they popped up. I'm wondering what the next step will be. It'll just happen when it happens.

Selected
Reading Lists

John Myerson

Alphabetical by author:

Bates, Brian, *Way of Wyrd,* Harper Collins, 1992

Bolen, Jean Shinoda, *Goddesses In Everywomen,* Harper, 1984

Bolen, Jean Shinoda, *Gods In Everyman,* Harper, 1989

Campbell, Joseph, *The Power of Myth,* Doubleday, 1988

Capra, Fritjof, *The Tao of Physics,* Shambhala, 1976

Castanada, Carlos, *Journey to Ixlan,* Simon & Schuster, 1972

Castanada, Carlos, *Tales of Power,* Simon & Schuster, 1974

· Eliade, Mercia, *Shamanism,* Princeton University Press, 1964

Erdoes, Richard, *Lame Deer, Seeker of Visions,*

     Washington Square Press, 1994

Ferrrucci, Piero, *What We May Be,* Tarcher, 1982

Grof, Stanislov, *Beyond the Brain,* SUNY Press, 1985

Harner, Michael, *The Way of the Shaman,* Harper & Row, 1980

Jung, C.G., *Memories, Dreams and Reflections,* Pantheon Books, 1963

Jung, C.G., *Dreams,* Princeton University Press, 1974

Kapleau, Philip, *The Three Pillars of Zen,* Beacon Press, 1965

Lame Deer, Archie Fire, *Gift of Power,* Bear & Co, 1994

Maslow, A., *Religions, Values and Peak Experiences*,

State University of Ohio, 1964

Nan, H.C., *Tao & Longevity, Mind-Body Transformation*, Weiser, 1984

Neuhardt, John, *Black Elk Speaks*, University of Nebraska, 196

Orr, L. & Ray, S., *Rebirthing in the New Age*, Celestial Arts, 1977

Perkins, John, *Psychonavigation*, Destiny Books, 1990

Perkins, John, *The World Is As You Dream It*, Destiny Books, 1994

Rank, O., *The Trauma of Birth*, Harcourt Brace, 1929

Salzberg, Sharon, *Lovingkindness*, Shambhala, 1997

Soygul Rinpoche, *The Tibetian Book of Living and Dying*,

Harper, SF, 1984

Starhawk, *The Spiral Dance*, Beacon, 1978

Suzuki, Shunryu, *Zen Mind, Beginner's Mind*, Weatherhill, 1970

Suzuki, Shunryu, *Not Always So*, Harper Collins, 2002

Tart, Charles, ed., *Transpersonal Psychologies*, Psychological Press, 1983

Van de Wettering, Janwillen, *The Empty Mirror*, Houghton Mifflin, 1973

Van de Wettering, Janwillen, *Glimpse of Nothingness*,

Houghton Mifflin, 1975

Whitaker, Kay, *The Reluctant Shaman*, Harper Collins, 1991

Robert Greenebaum

Alphabetical by author:

Brown, Tom, Jr., *The Vision*, Berkley Books, 1988

Calhoun, Marcy, *Are You Really Too Sensitive?*

    Blue Dolphin Publishers, 1990

Casteneda, Carlos, *A Separate Reality*, Washington Square Press, 1991

Casteneda, Carlos, *Journey to Ixtlan*, Washington Square Press, 1991

Casteneda, Carlos, *Magical Passes*, HarperPerennial, 1998

Casteneda, Carlos, *Tales of Power*, Washington Square Press, 1992

Casteneda, Carlos, *The Active Side of Infinity*,

    HarperCollinsPublishers, 1998

Casteneda, Carlos, *The Art of Dreaming*, Harper Perennial, 1993

Casteneda, Carlos, *The Eagle's Gift*, Washington Square Press, 1991

Casteneda, Carlos, *The Fire From Within*, Washington Square Press, 1991

Casteneda, Carlos, *The Power of Silence*, Washington Square Press, 1991

Casteneda, Carlos, *The Second Ring of Power*,

    Washington Square Press, 1991

Casteneda, Carlos, *The Teachings of Don Juan*, University of California

    Press, 1998

Casteneda, Carlos, *The Wheel of Time*, LA Eidolona Press, 1998

Chopra, Deepak, *The Way of the Wizard*, Harmony Books, 1995

Feledenkrais, Moshe, *The Potent Self*, Harper San Francisco, 1985

Hall, Judy, *The Karmic Journey*, Arkana, 1990

Halpern, Paul, *Time Journeys*, McGraw Hill, 1990

Hughes, James, *Altered States*, Watson-Guptill Publications, 1999

Hurbon, Laënnec (Trans. by Lory Frankel), *Voodoo*,

    Harry N. Abrams, Inc., 1995

Johnson, Robert A., *Inner Work*, Harper & Row, 1986

Johnson, Robert A., *Owning Your Own Shadow*,

    Harper San Francisco 1991

Keizan (Trans. by Thomas Cleary), *Transmission of Light*,

    North Point Press, 1990

Kim, Tae Yun, *Seven Steps to Inner Power*, New World Library, 1991

Miller, Willam A., *Your Golden Shadow*, Harper & Row, 1989

Mindell, Arnold, *Working on Yourself Alone*, Arkana, 1990

Narby, Jeremy, and Huxley, Francis, Editors, *Shamans Through Time*,

    Jeremy P. Tarcher/Putnam, 2001

Norwood, Robin, *Why Me, Why This, Why Now*,

    Carol Southern Books, 1994

Saunders, Nicholas J., *Animal Spirits*, Little, Brown & Company, 1995

Takuan Soho (Trans. by William Scott Wilson), *The Unfettered Mind,*
Kodansha International, 1986

Trungpa, Chögyam, *Cutting Through Spiritual Materialism,*
Shambhala Publications Inc., 1973

Vitebsky, Piers, *The Shaman,* Little, Brown & Company, 1995

Woolger, Roger J., *Other Lives, Other Selves,* Bantam Books, 1988